Mind how you handle me!

Mind how you handle me!

A New Testament protest

by
John C. King

HODDER AND STOUGHTON

Printed in Great Britain for Hodder and Stoughton
Limited, St. Paul's House, Warwick Lane, London, E.C.4
by Cox & Wyman, Ltd., London, Fakenham and Reading

Contents

Chapter One

Careful, that hurts !

Careful, that hurts! I know I look inoffensive on the shelf, but I don't enjoy being roughly handled any more than you do.

Oh dear, I'm going to be badly treated again. The real me is going to be well and truly hidden this time. He just wants to see a reflection of his own opinions as usual.

Well, if that's what you want, that's what you'll get.

No, he hasn't heard. He never hears *anything* when he's feeling like that. Ah well, I'll have to submit to being read *his* way. He'll find just what he wants to find in me—good as far as it goes, but nothing like the real thing.

Yet there's enough in my pages to cut the ground from under any man's feet. And not only ground. I'm sharp enough to cut like a scalpel. But this chap who's reading me now—he doesn't know that. He used to know something about it once—that's why he bought me in the first place—but he's forgotten now. I can remember how his eyes used to light up at the sight of me, but now they're lack-lustre and worn. I can see he doesn't expect to hear anything new; he thinks he knows it all already. And he's found a lot of other things to interest him more than his New Testament. Poor fellow! But I hear he's not the only one. That's why I've used some of my quieter moments (they're more frequent than they used to be) to rough out some notes on how things could be made better for both of us, my reader and me.

What's that? *You'd* like to have a look at the notes? Well, I suppose it will be all right. I wrote them for the benefit of my

9

owner really, but it seems that he's not going to take much interest in them. I can't get him to listen to me.

I said I was dangerous, didn't I? "Sharp" was the way I put it, if I remember. Sharper than any two-edged sword.[1] Exposing opinions and assumptions. Making the complacent uneasy. Frightening some people out of their lives. Frightening some people *into* their lives.

But, you know, the sharpest sword is quite harmless if it never leaves the scabbard. It might as well be a piece of wood. When people first get to know me they are glad I've got a cutting edge. They like to take me out of the scabbard. They respect me for what I am.

But over the years the effect wears off. When the enthusiasts grow older they become cautious and respectable. Instead of listening to what I say, they allow themselves to be guided by tradition. It's very sad for me. Here am I, with enough in me to make any molly-coddled worldling feel like a cat on hot bricks, and I am treated like a tailor's dummy in a shop window or a first edition in a glass case.

My trouble is that I have been around too long. It's fatal these days when everything worth-while is "new" and "advanced". It's no good being true or profound; you have got to be the latest. And I am not the latest by about nineteen centuries. I've got nothing "new" to say, even though "new" is part of my name and it's sometimes tickled me to think that I was "new" long before the copy-writers made "new" the official prestige adjective for your prosperous nineteen-sixties and nineteen-seventies.

No, I don't in the least mind having the distinction of being the oldest "new" product on the market, but I do sometimes get disheartened to think that the startling colours that I had when I started out have been toned down by carelessness and neglect into a dowdy mousiness that passes without any comment at all. It was a brilliantly-lit scene that brought me into being; now its impact has been neutralised. People think I've lost my edge or seen better days; it doesn't occur to them that human beings soon get bored with a new toy when the novelty wears off.

It's a strange thing. Men seem to find it the most difficult thing in the world to allow me to speak for myself. They distort what I

10

am trying to say and introduce modifications of their own just as though I was a production car asking to be souped-up. Almost the first claim made by any new religious movement inside the Christian Church is the claim that the movement is inspired by me. Me! I get blamed by neo-puritans, sabbatarians, corporal punishers and total abstainers. "It's all in the New Testament," they say. Without so much as a "By your leave"!

Swift knew what he was talking about. You remember that as well as *Gulliver's Travels* he wrote *Tale of a Tub*. He described very neatly the process by which a dying father's instructions to his sons were gently and gradually modified after his death until in the end there was nothing at all left of the intended pattern. What Swift was really writing about was the way people distort *me*. It makes me ache all over to think of the way I am constantly being wrenched and twisted to fit preconceptions and prejudices. It has been going on for so long now.

Sometimes there comes along a man who takes notice of what is happening. Usually he is a newcomer to the Church who has not been conditioned over the years to accept customary deviations and departures. For a short time he creates alarm and confusion by asking bluntly why the things that are done are so different from the things that are commanded in my pages. What happens next is that he is taken aside and persuaded that matters are not as simple as he thinks, that it is quite impracticable to do exactly what is prescribed in the New Testament, that there are a hundred and one considerations to be borne in mind, etc. etc.

I should be the first to agree that nobody in his senses could reasonably expect the Church as men know it today to be the same as the Church in my day. Men have made a certain amount of progress in nineteen hundred years. If they hadn't, I should still be copied out by hand each time some wealthy patron wanted a new copy of me. But some differences between the Church in my day and the Church in your day reflect not so much the advance of centuries as a type of development which has smothered me in a welter of vested interests, rigid conventions, ignorant speculation and wishful thinking.

Certain characteristics peculiar to my own age are plainly not to be repeated today. Nobody would wish the Church to have the

11

power to strike dead every Ananias who defaulted on his stewardship undertaking,[2] and nobody seriously expects bishops' handkerchiefs to have remarkable therapeutic powers.[3] But people are reasonable to expect the determining principles of the Church in my day and the Church today to be identical, even if details are different. I can't blame men for expecting to see the vigour and initiative of the apostolic age as much in evidence today as it was in the early days.

However, here he comes. He's got that weary look in his eyes as though reading me is a dull duty that has to be performed if a man wants to remain a believer. I know he doesn't enjoy opening me up, but I think this time I'll give him a surprise. You will excuse me, won't you? Instead of letting him just sit there and read me, I'll put some of these notes of mine into his head. Well, after all, I can but try. I'd like to see what happens when he's tingling with excitement instead of bored to tears at the prospect of opening his New Testament. Here goes, then.

Chapter Two

Do you know what I am?

I say there! Yes, I'm trying to say something to you if only you would listen. No, I know your hearing is not too good after all these years of coming to me for an echo of your own opinions, but there's something you ought to know.

You have had me on your shelf for a good many years now. You have turned to me more or less frequently all the time you have owned me. You have got into the habit of referring to me respectfully. But—and this is what has finally provoked me to break my silence—you are now bored with me. You take me for granted. You don't expect to hear anything new from me. You are—if you'll excuse my saying so—dull and perfunctory in your reading. Other things interest you more. I feel I'm wasting my time and yours.

So now, with your permission, I'm going to say my piece. No, don't be alarmed. There's nothing personal in this. What I'm going to say to you I could say to thousands of my readers. You're not the only one who misuses me.

Now, where shall we start? Let's start with a question: do you know what I am?

You look puzzled.

No comment?

Well, let me tell you what I'm *not*. I am not an encyclopaedia. I repeat: I am not an encyclopaedia.

What's that? You say you know that very well? All right then. If you know I am not an encyclopaedia, why do you treat me as though I am one?

15

You don't understand what I mean? Let me explain.

You're not the only one who gets this wrong. Lots of people who read me would protest at once that they know perfectly well I am not an encyclopaedia. But in fact they treat me like one.

Oh, I don't mean that they think my contents are arranged alphabetically or that they would reach for me instead of *Hutchinson's* if they wanted some quick information on Machiavelli or Sir Isaac Newton. They're not completely lacking in intelligence; they just don't know what I am. And that's where some people go astray right at the beginning.

So, with your permission, we'll start at the beginning. And I'll give you a general principle. If you want to understand a work of art or a piece of handiwork, you must know what it *is*. It's no good looking at a mosaic and grumbling because it does not have the delicate tones of a water-colour. Nor is it any good complaining that one of Constable's pictures is lacking in action and speed. If you want action and speed, the best thing to do is to go to a photographic exhibition with some fast shutter work on display—or better still go to a wide-screen movie film. You must know what a thing is before you can have any intelligent understanding of it.

You're still not quite clear about what I'm saying? Well, you have a boat, haven't you? Suppose somebody said that your catamaran (or whatever you call it) couldn't carry a hundredth part of what an old tramp steamer could carry. You would laugh at him, wouldn't you? You would point out that your boat wasn't designed to carry coal or cement or timber and that it was silly to expect it to. And you would be perfectly right. You accept your boat for what it is, a small, fast, highly manœuvrable vessel designed for three or four people. It serves your purpose well, you have lots of fun with it, but it would be completely unsuitable as a cargo vessel.

Well, now. It's just the same with me. If you want to get the best out of me, the first thing to get clear is what I *am*.

You look a little dazed. Am I going too fast for you, or is it that you're just not used to hearing what I've got to say? The real me has been suppressed so long, you know, that I'm afraid I come out like a champagne cork when I'm given the chance.

16

At the risk of boring you, I want to insist on this business of not being an encyclopaedia. So many people treat me as one that it has made me a bit sensitive on the point. People come to me expecting me to give them authoritative answers on church music, the upbringing of children, immigration policy and vegetarianism. But I am not that sort of book. I am not a comprehensive guide to all the questions that you believers happen to be interested in at any given moment. As an encyclopaedia I am a complete failure. My contents are not systematically arranged, I am not comprehensive, and I give quite disproportionate attention to matters which only ever had a limited, local application. Who nowadays is interested in butcher's meat offered to idols[4] and the different hair-styles favoured by men and women in first-century Corinth?[5]

You agree? Splendid. I can see you have got over that slight shock I gave you when you started listening to me. It slowed up your reactions, didn't it? Well, for every person like you who understands that I am not an encyclopaedia, there are dozens who don't understand at all. They think they are doing me justice by looking on me as a book full of religious information and definitive answers to all kinds of questions. They expect to find specific answers to their questions somewhere between Matthew and Revelation. And by hook or by crook they usually succeed in doing so. They ill-treat me dreadfully. It's like using a carving-knife to poke the fire; it can be done, but it is an insult to any self-respecting carving-knife.

All right then. You're prepared to agree that I am not an encyclopaedia and you won't come to me expecting to find the answers to all your questions. That's a real step forward. But you must be clear about the implications of this. You have to face the fact that lots of the most important issues in life are not so much as mentioned in my pages. There's next to nothing about democratic government, industrial problems, penal reform, education, the arts, leisure and a multitude of other things. On practical issues in these fields you must make up your own mind in the light of my basic teaching—and you won't all come to the same conclusions on such matters as capital punishment and comprehensive education.

So you won't think, will you, that just because a particular subject is not mentioned in my pages it is of no consequence? You won't restrict your interest to things that are in the New Testament, will you? I only say this because it sometimes happens that people who have a great respect for me seem to allow their natural curiosity to die. They stop asking questions about human nature, about the sun, the moon, the stars, daffodils, mountains, Troy, DNA and the Bill of Rights. A respect for me does not mean that an inquiring mind must become numbed or defunct. I was written—at God's prompting, true—by human beings, for human beings, and it is no sign of progress for a man to shut his mind to anything that is not mentioned in my pages. (By the way, I like the new colour-scheme you have chosen for your boat; I wish they would let you draw up a colour-scheme for that church interior where you sometimes take me.)

Very well then. I am not just an information-book, a book full of answers to questions asked by religious people.

Here's another thing I am *not*. I am not an examplar. You know what an examplar is: a model, a pattern, something to copy. I don't think you yourself make this mistake. But there are many people who do. They persuade themselves that if only believers today would copy the New Testament Church all would be well. What a thought! Emulate the Church of my day! If only they stopped to think about it, they would realise that such a course would be (*a*) impossible and (*b*) highly inadvisable.

Impossible? Yes, because there are so many gaps, so much that was never recorded in my pages. It's down in black and white, for instance, that young John Mark caused a row between Paul and Barnabas,[6] and possibly later he wrote down Peter's recollections of Jesus in the Gospel according to St Mark. But what happened to him after the row is something about which we know next to nothing. It's down in black and white that Apollos preached far better sermons after Mr and Mrs Eagle took him aside one day and pointed out what was missing in the message he was preaching.[7] But what happened to Apollos afterwards and whether Mr and Mrs Eagle often did this kind of thing we do not know. At least *I* don't. All I can give you is a number of tantalising references in I Corinthians.[8]

Another thing: I've got no record of the early believers being told to observe the first day of the week and I've certainly got no record of any instruction to move the sabbath from the last day to the first. A good many people hold the opinion that both these things are binding upon believers today, but it is an opinion for which I can scarcely be held responsible.

No, there are great glaring gaps in my record of the early Church. I'm not ashamed of it. There's quite enough to help you and all the others to find God, but there is not enough to make it possible to know exactly what the Church in my day was really like. If you must know, you will have to guess. I can't help you.

But even if it were possible to know exactly what the Church of my day was like, it would be inadvisable to attempt to copy it. I wasn't born in a Golden Age, you know. Exciting it may have been, dangerous, too, but the early Church was very far short of perfection. Think of the way Peter faltered, for example, over the question of admitting Gentiles. That brought about a clash with Paul.[9] Think of all those peculiar ideas some members of the early Church had—baptizing for the dead,[10] for instance, and showing off at services of worship.[11] Then there were those rival groups and factions,[12] each thinking it alone was right and all the others wrong. Very disturbing it was and sometimes rather unpleasant. No, I shouldn't advise anybody to emulate the Church of my day.

Except in this. Whatever mistakes the apostles and others made, they were adaptable and full of initiative. Thanks to the Holy Spirit, they did not allow themselves to get tied up in administration and committees and pettifogging details. They put first things first. They sought to glorify God and to make Christ known to Jew and Gentile alike. Think what happened when they found that some of their widows were being neglected. Seven men were appointed to what looks like a new order of ministry; some of your friends regard it as the beginning of the diaconate.[13]

Now this raises an interesting point, which you may have thought of before, but which may on the other hand be quite new to you. You remember the first humanists—Erasmus and Co.? Well, some of them thought that it was only when a word, or an inflexion, or a construction had actually been used by Cicero that it was legitimate to use it in Latin of their own; any new constructions were quite out of the question. That is what some men thought, and as a result Latin was killed as a living language. Other humanists went to Cicero not for precedents but for inspiration; they studied Cicero's prose carefully, applauded all that they judged to be excellent, and then sought to do as well as he had done in their own creative writing—without bothering to find precise Ciceronian precedents. You have to make up your mind whether you are coming to me for precedents (religious, not linguistic, of course) or for inspiration. If you come to me for precedents, you will be entirely guided by what the apostles themselves did and by the detailed directions they gave. If you come to me for inspiration you will expect to have your mind illuminated, your heart warmed and to shape your life by the guiding principles I contain. It may well be that the way you shape your life will be different from the way other believers shape theirs, but this is no more than you would expect if you recognise that you and all the others are poor fallible creatures doing your best to understand the will of God. You will be able to accept and indeed enjoy the variety without dreaming of a purely hypothetical universal agreement. Of course, you may on the other hand decide to come to me for precedents, but if you do I am afraid you are going to land yourself in serious trouble, and I should strongly advise against it.

Now, where was I? Ah yes, I was telling you what I am *not* as a preliminary to telling you what I *am*.

Imagine for a moment that you have a horse—yes, a horse. You are thinking of entering him for the Grand National. But you have overlooked one thing—what kind of horse it is. It is in fact a Shire. Now would you or anybody else want to enter a Shire for the Grand National? I thought you wouldn't. Odd, isn't it, how you human beings can tell the difference between a horse that is good over the sticks and a horse that is good at pulling brewers' drays, but you can't tell the difference between a book like me and an encyclopaedia.

I suppose it isn't so strange, though, that you have never given much thought to what I am. After all, lots of people go to an everyday book like a dictionary without recognising it for what it is. They expect to find authoritative rulings about spellings and meanings. They forget that one dictionary may give one spelling and another dictionary may give another. (Try looking up the spelling of a word like "likable" in more than one dictionary.) People like that do not know what a dictionary is any more than they know what language is, so it is hardly surprising that they do not know what a New Testament is.

Indeed, so blind are some people that—and I hesitate to mention this lest it should offend you, and I know you don't think this—they regard me as little more than a collection of adages, a source of wisdom like the *Rubaiyat* of Omar Khayyám, useful as a book of old saws for larding after-dinner speeches or man-to-man talks with growing boys, but useful for little else.

This makes my hair stand on end. This is misusing me with a vengeance. It's a bit like regarding your Rover 2000 as a source of spare parts. When you need a bit of wire or a bulb or a leather seat, you go to the garage and remove what you need. The car is never used as a car; it is a collection of accessories that happens to be standing on four wheels in the garage. I can see you're horrified. Well, I'm a New Testament and I expect to be treated as a New Testament. That means that I expect to be considered as one of the world's most important books, not a mere service counter with religious accessories on display. I ask, and I reckon I deserve, to be treated as a serious book. I ask to be regarded in my entirety, not to have bits and pieces taken out of me just as a reader fancies. But more of that later.

There now, I've told you what I am *not*. Now let me tell you what I *am*.

For one thing I am obviously a slice of early church life. What you find in my pages is a bundle of reports, letters and committee decisions. I know I am an untidy production with loose ends, higgledy-piggledy happenings, complaints, accusations, admonitions and high resolve. I am a brief account of the development of the early Church through a couple of generations. My compilers made no attempt to be comprehensive or systematic and they realised perfectly well that they were leaving many questions unanswered. The slice is a thin one.

Thin as the slice is, I reckon it is an eye-opener—if you'll forgive me for mixing my metaphors. In my pages is a record of a new dimension being discovered in everyday life, a dimension familiar enough in a way to the devout reader of the Old Testament but a dimension all too easily missed by a society which is preoccupied with practical matters. For a few moments in the history of mankind the curtain separating this world from its Creator was ripped apart and then sewn up again. Nothing can ever be quite the same afterwards. The glimpse some men caught galvanised them into writing down what they saw and heard.

Rough edges there may be to the revelation (Gospel-writers did not always check their facts and verify their references; nor did they collaborate in order to produce a tidy, dove-tailed account) but the rough edges attest the genuineness of the revelation and smack of the eye-witness haltingly recalling an incident for the man with notebook and pencil. Men of all generations have found that my pages have an air of authenticity.

Precarious it may be to balance two thousand years of civilisation on a few documents gathered together about the life and death of Christ, but this is the choice that you have to make once you decide to take me seriously. I should like to show you a way to avoid the dilemma, but I'm afraid I can't.

That's the kind of book I am—not a reference book serving up information when it's required, but a book that makes changes in men's outlooks. So watch out! Make sure you know what I am before you start reading me seriously or you may get an unhappy surprise.

Phew! I'm quite overcome. What a tiring business talking is! However do you human beings do so much of it? I think I'll get back on to the shelf and have a rest if you don't mind.

Chapter Three

Why blame the sextant?

Hullo! It's me again! You didn't think I'd finished, did you? Just because I'd convinced you I wasn't an encyclopaedia but a slice of early church life and a bit of an eye-opener, I suppose you thought that was all that needed saying.

Oh no, there's lots more. The next —

What was that you said? You promise never to mistake me for an encyclopaedia again? Good! I can see we're getting —

I beg your pardon. Did I hear you correctly? You like some parts of me better than others? Yes, you ought to look ashamed of yourself. Mind you, it doesn't surprise me in the least. I could have told you as much from the way some of my pages are still stuck together. But I ask you! Would you treat any other book this way, picking and choosing the parts you don't like and leaving the rest?

You would? Oh . . . Wordsworth, "The Prelude", and . . . Chaucer, the "Parson's Tale". Yes, you have a point there. I must admit you have a point. Perhaps I was over-stating my case. To put the matter in more moderate terms, then, is there any book of comparable importance that you would treat that way, picking and choosing, I mean? *Hamlet*, for instance, or Plato's *Republic*?

No? You agree that any serious book of reasonable length ought to be read in its entirety? Splendid. Of course it should. But it doesn't often happen like that.

I'll tell you what happens.

A young man gets to know a bunch of people of his own age

who are in raptures about a pet theme—perhaps conversion, or the fulness of the Spirit, or the Second Coming. With their help and guidance he starts reading me. Everywhere he looks he finds something about conversion, or whatever else it may be. He underlines verses, writes notes in the margin, asks his friends how they interpret what he has found. He becomes so caught up with this theme that he sees nothing else. He is a bit like some of those horsy friends of yours who call any dog which is not a fox-hound a "cur"—no matter what may be its merits at Cruft's. Unbalanced, that's what he is.

All right. Wait a minute. I'm not saying that it's wrong to rely on other people to help you get started on the New Testament. Other people's help is probably indispensable. It's true of other books and it's true of me that the novice must have a guide to put him on the right track. But he is foolish if he never goes anywhere without the guide, and he is a poor sort of fellow if he is content to see only what the guide is able to point out to him. If there's anything in him at all, he will want to explore for himself.

Mind you, exploring by yourself can have its surprises. I can think of lots of people who have been astonished to find the story of the coin in the fish's mouth[14] and the cursing of the fig tree.[15] It's not all plain sailing, but a nautical person like you would not expect plain sailing all the time. I wouldn't have those salt-water stains in the middle of Mark if you did.

Take the Second Coming. That's another part of me that is often unknown territory to seasoned readers—or perhaps I should say seasoned dippers. They have never stopped to consider that Jesus was not merely a great teacher and story-teller but a person who was filled with foreboding and uttered warnings about the end of everything. I know that the Second Coming has been discredited as far as many sensible people are concerned because it has been monopolised by people with a glint in their eye, but there is plenty about it in my pages. If you (I don't mean you personally; I mean all you human beings) ignore it, you are not doing justice to the documents in the case.

Put it this way. What was that sketch you were doing the other day? Nothing much? Just a lock-keeper's house and a lock-gate?

26

I remember. Now when you did that sketch you were a creator; you were making something that had never existed before. All right, it wasn't particularly good, but it was *your* work. *You* made it. Now one of the things you find in my pages is a reminder that a creator is one who begins *and ends* a job. When *you* do a sketch, you rub out lines as well as draw them. What is true about you as a creator is also true of God. He rubs out as well as draws. The end as well as the beginning is in his hands. Yet an extraordinary number of people read my pages and miss this point entirely. They will not acknowledge that the end is in God's hands, and that Jesus had a good deal to say about it. They take what they like from me and leave the rest.

Of course the thing that follows is Hell, and here again, people ignore what is as plain as a pikestaff. If there is one thing that you'll find if you read me thoroughly it's Hell.[16] The teaching of Jesus is quite emphatic about it and this embarrasses people. So they do what human beings usually do about an unpleasant fact (if they can, that is). They pretend it isn't there. . . .

Of course, when you human beings pick and choose, you make your selection on a purely personal basis. You pick out those bits of me that you like just as you yourself selected your car or your thornproof suit. Lots of other people make a selection in the same way. And because you human beings are much more like one another than you are prepared to admit, you often select pretty much the same bits and pieces. I'm not the only New Testament to have pages in Revelation still stuck together, you know, and I've got a feeling that those very clean pages in Hebrews are a fairly common phenomenon. Quite different from Luther—he would have cut James right out if he had had his way. But then Luther was quite different from other people all through his life, and Luthers aren't born every day.

What happens when you have individuals picking and choosing what they like out of my pages is that you get an infinite range of variations on the Gospel—some so distorted that I would altogether disclaim them—with a mass of vague, nondescript interpretations dominating the centre of the range.

Don't misunderstand me. I don't want to be a kind of dictator, telling people exactly what opinions they must hold on everything. But I do expect what every serious book expects, fair consideration, and that means taking me as I am. If people find bits in me they don't like or don't understand, they shouldn't make alterations in *me*; they should sit down and ask whether it isn't time to make alterations in their own opinions.

This, after all, is what I am for. I am not a department store which you human beings can visit as you please so as to take what you fancy from the shelves. I am an authoritative document. Once you start taking me seriously I expect *you* to change *your* opinions; I don't expect *you* to start changing *me*.

Put it this way. If you were to brush up your navigation and set off in your catamaran for Finisterre, you wouldn't blame the stars, or the sextant, or the nautical tables, if you one day fixed your position in the middle of the Sahara. You would accept the fact that the stars, sextant and tables were right and that you yourself had made a mistake in your deductions. This is exactly the way you have to treat me—not make corrections to me, but ask yourself whether you have made a mistake in your working.

If you think I am pitching my claims rather high, ask yourself what the alternative is. I think you will have to agree that it's a matter of every man having the kind of Christianity that suits him best. In my view it's best to reserve the description "Christianity" for the religion you find when you read me, all of me.

This does not, let me repeat, this does not mean slavish adherence to a book. It does not mean a dull uniformity among men and women in Christ. But it does mean that when people talk about Christianity they mean the same thing. It does mean that people are in agreement about the basic things, that they know where to go if they want fresh light and inspiration, if they want to take their bearings.

I think you will have to admit that I have suffered a good deal in this matter of picking and choosing. The people who like my well-known parables—the Good Samaritan, the Prodigal Son, etc.—and haven't much time for that saying of Jesus about giving his life a ransom for many,[17] they turn Christianity into a matter of benevolence and a helping hand. Usually they are excellent people, and I expect you would say that the world would be a far better place if there were more benevolence and more helping hands. But the spread of benevolence and helpfulness is not the same thing as the spread of Christianity, at least not the kind of Christianity found in my pages. It depends, you see, whether people take me seriously or not. If they want *my* kind of Christianity to flourish, they will have to take me as they find me—and that means an end to picking and choosing.

There is a kind of picking and choosing, however, which is not just a matter of individual preferences. Some picking and choosing is almost involuntary. It follows from the particular point of view that has been deliberately adopted by the people concerned. For instance, those who strongly advocate set forms of worship tend to turn a blind eye to the practice of the Corinthian Church.[18] Those who confuse Christianity with total abstinence forget that Jesus himself (unlike John the Baptist) drank wine, and made the drinking of wine a central feature of the worship of his new religion.[19] Those who make episcopal ordination an essential prerequisite of a Gospel ministry find more order in my pages than I have ever noticed myself.

When people have adopted particular standpoints like these, they hardly notice those passages which do not reinforce their views. They develop a kind of blind spot and impose their own interpretation on me despite my protests. This kind of thing is particularly noticeable among those who favour highly developed doctrinal systems. A man may lay great emphasis upon the need for church order and continuity and as a result be hardly aware of the free benefits offered to all men on the basis of Christ's death on the Cross. On the other hand, a man may be so preoccupied with this latter point that he sees the whole of me in forensic terms—in terms, that is, of the law court.

It may be worth spending a moment on this so as to see how this blind spot develops.

It is quite true that if you read me at all carefully you will find that one of the most important interpretations of the death of Christ that I have to offer is an interpretation in legal terms. Man has committed an offence against his Creator and law-giver; he is accused, found guilty and sentenced; Christ's death, however, wipes out the offence and makes it possible for the

29

offender to be acquitted.[20] Now nobody in his right senses could deny that this interpretation is important, but some people become so enthusiastic about it that they see nothing else in me at all. They hardly notice that Jesus gave a central place in his teaching to the matter of his kingdom. They forget the stress which I lay upon human beings sharing in Christ's death and resurrection through baptism.[21] They forget my stress on the energy and drive imparted by the Holy Spirit.[22] They allow their whole attention to be focused on this one—admittedly very important—line of teaching. They quite involuntarily allow their outlook to become totally unbalanced.

Now one practical outcome of this can be seen in the way believing parents sometimes approach the upbringing of their children. The parents themselves have been conditioned by a persuasive minister to see God as primarily a God who makes laws and inflicts punishment. Retribution, inflicted or withheld, is the key to their religion. And—let there be no doubt about it— they are entirely sincere and well-intentioned in the practice of it. But the result is that their relationship with their children tends to express itself in a pattern of laying down laws and inflicting or withholding punishment (often, I am sad to say, corporal punishment). The idea of understanding, encouraging and gently directing little people is foreign to parents like this. They regard their offspring as morally responsible beings, as miniature adults, and they treat them accordingly. It is heavy-handed treatment like this that has blighted many a tender young life and I am afraid that an unbalanced type of Christianity must be held responsible.

A moralising interpretation of Christianity is better, I suppose, than the old amoral religions with their Bacchanalian revels, but it is a gloomy Gospel when overdone, and I sometimes wonder whether the lack of initiative and curiosity that you tend to find among the thoroughgoing adherents of the condemnation and acquittal school must be laid to its account.

That's just one example. What I am really saying is that to treat me as a whole, to refuse to pick and choose, is a very severe discipline. I perfectly well understand your finding some parts of me more interesting than others. This is to be expected. But the

30

fact that you find one or two particular parts of me more helpful than other parts does not necessarily signify that those one or two parts are extraordinarily important. It may mean that your judgement is defective. And it's not taking me seriously to stick to the bits you happen to like. All right, I may seem muddled and contradictory. But give me a chance. Look at me a bit more closely and see whether the mistake is not of your making. Remember what I said about the stars and the sextant. You have got to be very sure of yourself before you say the stars are wrong. Have you really read me so thoroughly that you can be quite sure that I am wrong and not you?

Hm! You're looking thoughtful. I think I'll leave you now and get back to my shelf.

Chapter Four

You see what you expect to see

Ah!, you're back! You've been to do a bit of shopping? In the supermarket? Well, that's a good place to start. . . . No, not about picking and choosing, about something different this time —but just as important.

If you were to ask your wife where the cheese was on display she would be able to tell you at once. My guess is that she visits that particular section every time she borrows the car and goes to stock up. It might take her a moment to find just the piece of Double Gloucester or Wensleydale that she thinks you might fancy, but she could march straight to the cheese department without any hesitation.

But *you* are different. You might be able to go straight to the licensed section and ask for a bottle of rosé, but you would be lost as far as the soap powders, tea, butter and tinned mushrooms are concerned.

No, I *don't* think you go around with your eyes shut, but I know that like all the other human beings—except perhaps for somebody as exceptional as Sherlock Holmes—you see what you expect to see.

Take your friend Bill, the traffic engineer. When he crosses by those lights near the supermarket I'm sure he is often thinking about the better use that could be made of the road space if only more lanes and arrows were painted on the surface, whereas the schoolboy crossing the road has eyes for nothing but the shop selling the fishing tackle. And you yourself, because you're an architect, you observe things in the High Street that nobody else notices at all.

It's obvious really, isn't it. You notice what you have been trained to notice. You're blind to the things that don't matter to you. You see what you expect to see.

It's true of books as well, and it's particularly true of me. People read all kinds of ideas back into me because they come to me expecting to find them. They fill in all those gaps I mentioned earlier with their own assumptions, and then they blame me for something that has been in their heads all the time.

I know I can't expect you to come to me with a completely blank mind. Inevitably you bring your background, your previous reading—a hundred and one things—to any book you propose to read. But if you are going to get the maximum benefit from me or any other book you have to recognise your own assumptions and discard the ones that are inappropriate before you start on page one.

You, for instance, come to me as a knowledgeable, youngish man with a well-ordered family, a responsible job and a discriminating taste. You also come as an inheritor of the western European traditions shaped by Christendom. I beg your pardon, I should have said "what is left of the western European traditions shaped by Christendom". I well know that your generation is moving away from those traditions and exploring the idea of an open society with different boundary lines. Those humanist friends of yours don't let the grass grow under their feet. But, even before you began to read me a few years ago, you were still shaped and influenced by the traditional Christian way of thinking.

Furthermore, you have other difficulties. People like you have been brought up to admire (if they have been brought up to respect religion at all) a form of religion that is moderate, hardly supernatural, and that puts an emphasis on hymn-singing, doing your best and generally decent behaviour. If I may say so without offence, your temperament, insular, pragmatic, amateurish—delightful though it is—is a thousand miles removed from the cosmopolitan, peasant origins of Christianity. So is the residue of religion that you and millions of others like you have inherited—

stained glass rather than mosaic, change-ringing rather than ikons, Bible class rather than sacrament. It's all so deeply ingrained that you don't notice it.

Don't forget that I first saw the light of day when the majority of the inhabitants of the civilised world were slaves. Most men had no choice in their rulers and they had never heard of romantic love, feudalism, capitalism or nationalism. Persians, Egyptians and Scythians were near neighbours. The Atlantic was an unexplored sea of frightening dimensions. The mysterious east was a source of spices and legends. Africa was unexplored beyond the cornfields on the edge of the Mediterranean.

Now *you* flew home across the Atlantic the other day. You married the girl of your choice (and her choice). Africa is well and truly explored, mostly independent states and on the way to industrialisation. It is going to take a big effort of the imagination for you to come to the job of reading me in the way my first readers did. How can you, with your tidy, compartmentalised approach to life, understand the outlook of men for whom the supernatural was always round the corner, with the gods expected to appear at any moment?

When you read that story by Jesus about hired hands being paid arbitrary and inequitable wages by an employer with a stunted sense of responsibility,[28] you are indignant, so indignant that you find it impossible to discern any message about God's dealings with men and women. But if you are expecting the spirit of the negotiating table to appear amongst Mediterranean peasants 2,000 years ago, you are being quite unrealistic. Remember what happened to the Tolpuddle martyrs as recently as 1834. It is only during the past century that you have grown accustomed to a steady campaign for better working conditions. When Jesus told that story about labourers in the market-place, he was making a point about God's generosity; he was not raising the question of fair working conditions; that question was covered— for those who had eyes to see—by the Golden Rule. Had Jesus attempted to carry his listeners too far too quickly, he would have instigated not patient pressure by responsible proletarian leaders but a slave revolt of the kind led by Spartacus.

What's that you say? Why did Jesus accept outrageous conditions in human society? Well, I can't pretend to know, but perhaps it was because he was a realist and he knew that every person who seeks reform by methods depending upon consent must be patient and work within the limits imposed by his audience. I think Paul's letter to Philemon shows the same awareness. You remember, Paul did not attack slavery as such, but if Philemon had followed Paul's advice about his own slave and if that kind of thing had happened at all widely, slavery would have been finished.

It's no good reading your generation's ideas back into my pages. I can't help you if you do that. Take the question of relations between the sexes in your generation. A man and a woman make up their own minds whether they respect and are attracted to one another. In varying degrees they may be prepared to be guided by an overwhelming weight of emotion when it comes to making up their mind about a permanent union. They look forward in marriage to a lifetime of sharing and mutual enrichment. No girl today expects to be a man's skivvy; instead she must be his sweetheart, his partner, his companion, his bed-fellow, a hostess to the visitors, a mother to the children. In addition she will probably pursue a career of her own.

To bring this kind of conception to the New Testament is to ask to be misled. In my day the place of women was very different from what it is today. Male Greeks and Romans had respectable wives and mothers and looked elsewhere for sexual enjoyment—among prostitutes or young men. No Greek or Roman would expect a respectable woman to take any responsible or even intelligent part in the affairs of the world. Political activity would be an unknown game to women.

Among the Jews the position of women was both more and less burdensome. No Jewish woman would be allowed to marry outside her own nation; nor would she be allowed to marry the man of her choice. (Since romantic love had not yet been invented, this would not be the intolerable burden it might seem; a Jewish girl would be perfectly happy to leave it to her father.) She would be entirely dependent upon her husband; if he wished to divorce her, he had only to write a bill of divorce and hand it to her. If a bride was found to be less than a virgin on her wedding night, she was liable to be stoned to death; bridegrooms, on the other hand, faced no similar penalty. There was one law for the male, another law for the female. But a Jewish girl could reasonably expect her husband to be faithful to her and she could reasonably expect him not to show homosexual tendencies.

Seen in this light, references in my pages to the behaviour of women in church services[24] begin to make sense, don't you agree? It was not a matter of crushing hesitant steps to emancipation; it was rather a matter of prudently protecting a young religious movement from its best friends—those who wished to work out the implications of the new Gospel without any delay, whatever social upheavals might result. You have to recognise that the Gospel burst into a world in which men were smugly content with a state of affairs which gave them an unquestioned superiority over their wives and sisters. Men had the whip-hand and were happy to keep it so. You male human beings! You've got a lot to answer for over the centuries.

What's that? You agree with all I am saying? Well, all I can say is that you're different from lots of the people who read me. They come to me to be fortified in their views of male supremacy and they go away happily quoting St Paul on women keeping silence. But they forget the other things Paul said—about there being no male or female in Christ. I'm always half-expecting some of my readers to clamour for the re-introduction of slavery. If they favour sex discrimination, I really don't see why they shouldn't favour discrimination between slaves and freemen and between the different races. What Paul says is that all these distinctions are done away in Christ.

On this question of sex discrimination people are very reluctant to change opinions they have held for ten or twenty years, no matter what I say. Indeed, very often they simply can't see what is there on my pages. They're too preoccupied with what they know already. Their minds are made up.

What was that? I thought I heard something. Oh! Your door chimes. Of course I'll excuse you. . . .

*　　　*　　　*

It was a *what*? A market research interviewer? I know—one

39

of those people who come and ask you all sorts of questions about the television programmes you watch and the soap powder you use.

That reminds me of another way I get misunderstood. People are so conditioned by habits and market pressures that they can't believe Jesus meant what he said about looking at the lilies of the field and the birds of the air. I know very well you human beings have to make provision for your old age. You have to plan ahead for your children. You have to pay insurance premiums. But isn't there just a chink in your relentless programme when you can think about the carefree—I almost said happy-go-lucky—life that Jesus talked about in the Sermon on the Mount? The fact that you're listening to me now shows that you yourself find time for contemplating. And the fact that you have got some oil-paints and a battered typewriter in your study tells me that you find time for creative activity.

In my day people thought a lot of detachment and wisdom. They weren't always rushing from one thing to another. They wanted to know how they could please God. They wanted to live a full life. They found poetry around them where your generation finds television jingles. They lived close to the earth where you live close to print and television screen. They had time to commit things to memory and to relish works of literature; you are rushed helter-skelter from one catch-penny topic to another. They were bound together by great annual rituals like the Passover; all you have to bind you together is the winter binge and a favourite football team. They admired the mature man, the man who had learned wisdom over the years; you admire the executive, the man who gets things done.

No, I *don't* mean you personally. I get a bit carried away sometimes. I'm trying to point out the great difficulty a person of your generation has in trying to get the essential message from my pages without colouring it with his own preconceptions. I tell you, I've been ill-used so often that I know what I'm talking about.

People come to me thinking they already know what I'm going to say. Some of them regard religion as a purely inward matter, a private opinion, a view of life which may or may not be shared

40

by any other individual and is certainly not for public discussion. Others regard it as almost wholly an ethical matter—a habit of working to the Golden Rule,[25] or of putting into practice as much of the Sermon on the Mount as they consider practicable. Others regard it as a matter of taking part in certain stylised acts or procedures in special buildings.

Nobody—least of all myself—could say that these aspects of religion are entirely false or misleading, but they are quite frivolous if they are regarded as summing up my message. People who hold these views are deceiving themselves if they think that they are accepting the message to be found in my pages.

In my day people weren't nearly so conceited. They did not convince themselves that they had a religion because they had some half-formed notions floating in their heads; they knew that they had to choose from several specific brands. In the east was Zoroastrianism. The Romans could offer the official pantheon, the household gods and Caesar-worship. The more sceptical could settle for Stoicism; the "with it" could choose Mithraism. It was clear and precise. You had to make a definite choice.

Now a definite choice is just what many of your contemporaries want to avoid, as far as religion is concerned. They don't really want to think clearly about it at all. The fact that much of what passes for Christianity is no more than camouflaged Stoicism demonstrates this. Many people want everything to remain vague, and so when they come to consider me and my message they find just what they expect to find—vagueness and an absence of definite choices. But—though I say it myself—this is not me at all. Think of the choice between the broad way and the narrow way.[26] Think of the contrast between the sheep and the goats.[27] Think of my insistence on the difference between being outside Christ and being in Christ.[28]

I know I'm asking a lot of your generation. You are meticulous about space-travel and do-it-yourselfery, but unbelievably woolly-headed about religion. What I'm asking you to do is to clear your minds of misconceptions that may have coloured your religious outlook since childhood. I'm asking you to come to me with an open mind.

41

For most people this represents as great a mental upheaval as would be necessary if you were to change from the decimal system to the duodecimal system. But, unless this is recognised, and unless the clearance takes place, you will never understand me as you should. I know it is enormously difficult. I wish I could spare you the discomfort. However, I can't. As they say in examination instructions, this is one of the questions that must be attempted.

Chapter Five

Clearer than clear

First of all have a look at that newspaper on your desk. It's got a name, hasn't it? It's also got a headline—lots of headlines, in fact. Now what do you think is the function of a headline? . . .

Yes, quite. To give an indication of what a "story" is about, to compress what is probably quite a complicated matter into a few words. Obviously there's no room for subtleties or qualifications. Words like "blast", "slam", "scare" are at a premium. You can't blame a sub-editor for putting the matter baldly, crudely even.

It's not only sub-editors who have to simplify. Teachers give their children a general rule—about 'i' before 'e' for example— and immediately have to follow it with exceptions. That doesn't mean the rule is no good; it's a case of observing a broad outline and then noting exceptions.

It's not wrong to simplify. It's the only way to get to grips with complicated matters. *Janet and John* is simplified English and you don't complain because your three children are learning their English from *Janet and John*, do you? Of course not. But you *would* complain if they never advanced beyond *Janet and John*, wouldn't you?

That's the point. For the benefit of beginners lots of things— including the New Testament—have to be simplified. There's no other way of doing things. But if you stick to the simplified version after you have stopped being a beginner, you are not doing justice either to yourself or to me.

What's that you say? Am I feeling well? I'm all right, thank you, but it always makes me shiver to think of being simplified.

I know that some things—like dripping—need clarifying, but to do a "clearer than clear" transformation of a serious book like me robs me of all my dignity. When it happens I feel I am being turned into something else altogether. Perhaps it's because I've been thinking of that that I don't feel quite myself at the moment.

No, there's nothing you can do to help, thank you very much. Actually I don't feel at all bad when I know it's being done for the benefit of children. I'm on very good terms with the Ladybird books, for example; it's when I'm simplified for people who ought to have got beyond a simplified interpretation that I feel so bad.

Let me make myself clear. I'm not complaining about what you might call translations into the modern vernacular. Even *God is for Real, Man* is done in a good cause, for beginners, adult beginners. What makes me unhappy is the kind of simplification, *over*-simplification, I suppose I should say, that permanently reduces my message to a kind of A B C level with all the subtleties removed.

If that doesn't sound a very serious offence, try imagining what it would be like asking an artist to work in primary colours alone, or asking a poet to stick to basic English. Or think what it would be like swopping the engine in your Rover for a cheap engine with half as many crankshaft bearings and valves that didn't close properly. After all, it is only subtleties that distinguish a Rolls-Royce from a lesser car. To the superficial observer the two look more or less the same—four wheels, windscreen, headlamps, number-plates. It is only a mechanic who could point out precisely what is implied by finer tolerances and attention to detail. What would satisfy an engineering ignoramus would make a mechanic wince.

Now the difference between me as I am and me after the simplifiers have been at work is not something you would notice at first glance. But to simplify me is to ruin me. It is like turning a delicately balanced piece of engineering into a crude contraption that rattles and vibrates.

Why should people want to do a thing like that to me, you ask? I'll tell you. They think they are doing me a service, and

46

they think they are preserving my message in all its purity. But they're not. They're distorting me! In some ways I'd rather be ignored altogether.

You'd like some examples? Well, at one point inside my covers you'll find the words "Come out and be separate".[29] Paul wrote these words to urge his readers to have no truck with idols and false religions. But subsequently these words were applied to human society in general. Without any thought of those places where believers are said to be salt (fighting the decay in society) or are encouraged to fulfil their responsibilities as citizens, some people interpreted Paul's words as meaning that believers should shun all their fellow human beings who were not believers.

You can imagine the effect of this kind of simplification. Yes, precisely. Husbands separated themselves from their wives, men and women refused to take degrees and professional qualifications. Believers retired into little cliques and shut themselves off from society.

You smile. I know that it hasn't gone to those extremes amongst your particular friends. You have too much of a sense of humour for that. But the trends are there just the same. How many of your friends still have qualms about going to the theatre, or taking an interest in fashion, or using cosmetics, because at one time these things were taboo?

One of the key-words in the simplification process was "worldliness". "Worldliness" was regarded as undue attachment to a world which was seen as enemy-occupied territory. Particular activities were regarded as so imbued with "worldliness" that the only possible course was to abstain from them altogether. It was quite overlooked that whereas this view made the order of the day "Repudiate", my word was "Discriminate". It was discrimination, for example, that Paul prayed might become a characteristic of the Philippians.[30]

The result of this over-simplification was the withdrawal of many good people from the responsibility to be critical and creative within their own culture. They left culture to the unbelievers. Inevitably two things happened: the culture increasingly reflected an unbeliever's viewpoint, and the believers developed into Philistines, with no sense of good or bad in the arts.

What happened in the arts happened in secular responsibilities in general. It became acceptable to serve on the committee of a missionary society and unacceptable to serve on the local council. There was a quite improper renunciation of secular responsibilities by the man in Christ which brought no credit at all to the God whom he thought he was thereby serving.

The result of this "holiness by subtraction" trend was to make believers dull, grey and sometimes repulsive. It's not surprising. The man who trains himself to suspect and renounce the things he really enjoys (the pleasures, that is, that do not leave a trail of regrets and remorse) is in effect denying his true self; he is not making himself more holy; he is making himself less human. The logical end is that the world is divided into two—bigoted and censorious Christians and open-minded and creative unbelievers. The two groups do not overlap, and in the absence of any exchange of ideas evangelism is out of the question.

I'm glad to see you shudder. But these things do happen, you know, and almost invariably I get blamed for them.

If I remember rightly, my message is that men and women are to be transformed; but when the subtle matter of living a redeemed life in a fallen world is crudely and barbarously simplified, the result is not transformation but conformity. Instead of making up his own mind on particular issues, the believer finds himself rigidly applying group rules worthy of the Medes and Persians. The curious thing is that this type of legalistic conformity tends to characterise those who are most strongly opposed to legalism as a means of attaining salvation. Instead of exuberance and adaptability you have the grim determination of a man following the party line through thick and thin. The corollary is a stodgy, predictable type of personality, developed—if that is the right word—over the years by people who are no more delightful and attractive human beings at forty than they were at twenty. The risk-taking, adventurous religion called Christianity becomes a matter of playing safe and keeping up—or down—with the religious Joneses.

"Worldliness" is not the only area where over-simplification does enormous damage. Ministry is another. In my day there was, as far as I understand the matter, great diversity in ministry. There were apostles, prophets, teachers, miracle-workers, healers, helpers, administrators, speakers in various kinds of tongues.[31] This pattern easily gets over-simplified into a matter of a full-time professional who is expected to be good at everything and bear all the responsibility in a local church. Of course it is more efficient in a local church (as in nation-state) to have one boss than it is to have a variety of leaders, but efficiency in a church is not everything. You human beings lose something when you look on ordinary believers as sheep and a special class of believers as shepherds.

Or take evangelism. There was over-simplification here. People read me and discovered that one of their most pressing responsibilities was to bring the Gospel to other people. Very good. But they went on from there to conclude that it was the most pressing responsibility of all, that it came before worship and before a man's responsibilities as husband and father.

The result of this was that the Gospel was stood on its head. God became an auxiliary (a very powerful auxiliary, it is true) in the task of bringing men and women into salvation. Prayer became a matter of asking God to help in the work. Worship became little more than a suitable introduction to the task of preaching the Gospel. The first question in drawing up a programme for an evangelistic meeting became not "What will glorify God?" but "What will bring outsiders to a state of readiness to hear the Gospel?" The tawdry results of such a policy can be imagined.

Things are made clearer than clear when you human beings choose to use your own expressions rather than mine. Take the word "Christian". It occurs only three times in my pages, but you human beings bandy it about freely. You talk about "Christian" countries, "Christian" books, "Christian" organisations. It's a word that causes endless confusion, especially when it is indiscriminately applied as an adjective.

There are some groups of believers who have adopted this word into a private vocabulary which they share with like-minded people. They use it to mean a person who has had a religious experience similar to their own. Sometimes they qualify it in such an expression as: "He's a real Christian", or they even say: "He's a Christian in our sense of the word." The really damaging thing about using the word "Christian" in this way is that it is not only vague; it is loaded. To talk in this way is to suggest that to become a Christian it is necessary to accept a whole range of opinions and habits which, far from being taken from me, are traditional and provincial. If you want to be precise you may talk about people who (*a*) believe in the resurrection of Christ, or (*b*) are baptized. I can understand these terms; they are my own. I cannot understand what people mean when they use this word "Christian" so freely.

What was that you said? You've never really thought about the word "Christian" in this way? You can't think how they managed without it? I'll tell you. They managed without the word "Christian" because they had very much better words to use. People who acknowledged Jesus as Lord are described as disciples, brethren, believers, saints. They are said to be "of the Way",[32] to be calling upon the name of the Lord,[33] to be obedient to the faith.[34] Paul, giving an account of his own life, never said he became a Christian. He said he was apprehended by Christ,[35] he obtained mercy,[36] he became a man in Christ.[37] These terms are much richer—and far more searching—than the word "Christian". Perhaps they are too searching for you human beings to use every day. But I think you would do better if you stuck to my words rather than used an over-simplified, shorthand expression that is thin and loose.

"Be converted," is an expression of similar emptiness which has been made to bear an impossible burden. If you were offered five shillings for every time this word occurred in my pages, you would be doing well to get two pounds ten shillings. A man can be converted (it means no more than "turn") to almost anything —Buddhism, Conservatism, shaving with an electric razor. "Turn" is a colourless, neutral term. Its shallowness can be seen when it is set against another biblical word like "repent" or "regenerate". Man repents, God regenerates. There is a wealth of meaning there.

But sometimes, as I say, you human beings fight shy of words full of meaning. You talk about "becoming a Christian" and "being converted" when there are far better words to use.

50

Incidentally it is interesting to see how many expressions *are* used—which is an indication that it is not the straightforward matter it appears to be. When people asked Peter what they ought to do in response to the new teaching he had announced on the day of Pentecost, he replied: "Repent and be baptized".[38] He invited them to change their minds, to do what the prodigal son did—you remember, he "came to himself". That isn't just changing your opinion; that's changing yourself. You human beings can't just decide to repent whenever you feel like it, just as you may decide to have a drink of water or a breath of fresh air. It just isn't as simple as that. Something deep in you responds to pressure from outside. It happens when the moment is ripe.

Another thing people do by way of over-simplifying me is to smooth out my rough edges. Yes, I know they're there, and by this stage you ought to be able to recognise them for yourself. Look at the first verse or two of Mark's Gospel, for instance. Misquoting an Old Testament writer may not be the worst offence a man can commit (as John Calvin had common sense enough to realise), but it does imply that you should be extremely careful about using words like "infallible" to describe me. Similar imprecision is found in the different accounts provided by the writers of the Gospels. How many blind men, for example, were given sight outside Jericho when Bartimaeus called out to Jesus? No good service is performed by multiplying incidents or torturing the text in the interest of preserving a 100 per cent record of accuracy for the Gospel-makers; you have to recognise that you have differing accounts of some episodes and that you will never know the precise details. But these are no more than the rough edges of the revelation; they enhance the substantial authenticity and reliability of my record. In fact, I'm rather proud of my rough edges and I'm not very grateful to people who try to pretend that they are not there.

The over-simplifiers tend to gloss over the moral difficulties that I contain. Admittedly I do not contain any record of God commanding the slaughter of men, women and children in occupied cities, but I have my moral difficulties, none the less. When Jesus cured the demoniac at Gadara, he is said to have sent the evil spirits into near-by pigs.[39] It is probably only the fact that they were pigs and not cats or dogs that has restrained the pet-lovers from rejecting Christianity wholesale. But the problem remains. To human beings who accept responsibility for animals there must appear to be an element of arbitrary handling of animal life that is difficult to reconcile with responsible government of the created order.

If a man accepts the Gospel of God's free grace, he is often tempted to over-simplify questions of church order, perhaps even to treat the Church as of no importance whatsoever. I am told I am paradoxical on this point. On the one hand I advance the doctrine of justification by faith alone, and on the other hand I give a good deal of space to questions connected with the organising of the Church. They say it takes a bigger man to live with paradoxes than to live with crystal-clear formulations. They say the discipline of suspending final conclusions and being content with provisional answers is a mark of maturity, of Christian maturity as much as any other. Truth is something that eludes the grasp of you human beings, no matter how prehensile your intellect, it is said. Well, you must decide that for yourself.

I'll tell you how I sum it up. You can no more simplify me than you can simplify *Hamlet*. To simplify is to betray. To perpetuate an over-simplification for the benefit of people who ought to be thinking for themselves is monstrous. Each generation must be allowed to come to me expecting God to say new and disturbing things. My delicate balance should not be upset by misguided attempts to make me clearer than clear.

I think I'll go and have a rest now.

Chapter Six

Have you seen my first stage?

I've got a question for you. No, not about what I've told you already. It's up to you whether you take any notice of an old thing like me. No, I was going to ask you what your wife would say if you told her you were going in a rocket to the moon. . . .

She'd probably be very glad? How very—oh! I see! You've got your tongue in your cheek! Well, of course, I don't understand how husbands and wives treat one another these days, so I miss these little digs. Marriage customs were different in my day.

No, don't apologise. I'm not at all upset really. . . .

She would be alarmed? Very well. Let's go on from there. I guess that she would be even more alarmed if she knew that you were going to economise by doing without the first stage of the rocket. . . .

She would positively forbid you? And you wouldn't be too keen yourself? No. Quite. Little as I understand rockets, I know you can't do without the first stage, no matter how good the second stage may be.

I'll put it plainly. I'm only the second stage. There's a first stage too. When did you last have a look at it?

What it comes to is this: it is my job to describe the second stage of God's project to lift mankind out of ignorance and confusion. The "New" of New Testament is a relative term, for the Gospel is a development—a surprising development, in some respects, it is true—of something that had been familiar for a long time. In its way Christianity is like an advanced car with a

55

recognisable pedigree going back through earlier models. If you want to understand Christianity, the second stage, thoroughly, you must understand the previous stage—and that means you must understand the Old Testament. I don't know whether you have had many chats with him in the way you've discussed things with me, but I'm sure he'd agree with me.

Put it this way: you're fond of music, aren't you? When you put on a record of one of Beethoven's symphonies, you don't place the stylus very carefully each time so as to cut out the first movement, do you? Of course you don't. It's an integral part of the work.

Well, if you treat the first movement of a Beethoven symphony with respect you ought to treat the first stage of God's repair project with respect. If you wouldn't dream of considering the second stage of a rocket in isolation, as though there wasn't such a thing as a first stage, you shouldn't consider me in isolation. The Old Testament, remember, is not optional reading for believers in the Gospel; it is the first stage of the entire project.

The first stage was the selection and shaping of a particular race, the Jews. With Abraham God made an agreement. Abraham was promised untold descendants, and God said he would be their protector. Through generation after generation God tirelessly taught the members of this particular nation. He gave them Law (the Ten Commandments); he outlined a way of forgiveness (the tabernacle and its services); he gave them a succession of men (the prophets) who provided detailed—and often painfully pointed—progress reports.

You may ask why God should have to work to limitations like this. Why should there be any need for all this first stage work? Why could not Christ do all that was necessary straightaway? The answer is, so I believe, that God chose to work to these limitations because he loved these creatures called human beings and wanted to lift them to the heights without turning them into something else. He had to work *gradually*.

To put it in terms of school life, it was as though the ground-work had to be covered thoroughly before the A level work could be undertaken. First things had to come first. *Janet and John* had to come before syntax and semantics.

You won't need me to remind you that early in their victory the Jews had become horrified by the religious practices of their national neighbours. As a result they had erected strong barriers to prevent their own religion from being corrupted. They found every encouragement to do so in their religious literature and particularly in the section called the Law. Minute regulations were laid down in Leviticus and Deuteronomy about what was clean and what was unclean. It was permissible, for example, for Jews to eat salmon but not eels, beef but not bacon. Sexual intercourse made you "unclean"; so did touching a dead body.

Over the years these regulations about uncleanness were tightened up until it became an accepted thing that a Jew was not permitted even to enter the house of a non-Jew for fear of defiling himself. The defilement was recognised as a ceremonial one, but it was none the less meaningful for that. In practice it meant that the Jewish faith was on the brink of becoming purely external, a matter of conforming to a code of do's and don'ts rather than a matter of attitude. Conformity rather than charity, law rather than love, summed it up.

In this setting Jesus appeared to the religious leaders of the day as a trouble-making revolutionary. He flouted the regulations which the religious leaders had scrupulously worked out to the last detail. He upset the clear distinction between clean and unclean, between Jew and Gentile. He healed a Roman soldier's batman,[40] he healed the daughter of a Syrophoenician woman.[41] He prodded his friends into taking a similar view. Peter, you remember, hesitated and half-rebelled when he had a vision followed by an instruction to enter a Gentile's house soon after Jesus had died and risen.[42] When you think of the disruptive effect of Jesus' teaching on the carefully elaborated pattern fostered by the Jews, you cannot be surprised that their leaders set about plotting his downfall.

How anybody can understand this by reading me alone, without any attention to the Old Testament, I do not know. As far as I can see, it just can't be done.

Or again, think of what John the Baptist says at the beginning of Jesus' ministry: "Behold the Lamb of God!"[43] What can anybody make of this if he has never heard of sacrificial lambs or the Passover? I mentioned the Syrophoenician woman a moment ago. Perhaps you remember that Jesus told her that he had come to help only the lost sheep of the house of Israel. What can a man make of this if he does not understand that God had treaty obligations, as it were, towards the Jews? I could quote dozens of examples to show that without some understanding of the Old Testament a man cannot possibly get the most out of the New.

When Christ discussed points with the Jews, he was exchanging ideas with men who already had strong convictions about God as the Creator and the giver of the Law. This is why they were offended when he forgave sins and interpreted the Law in what appeared to them to be an eccentric and high-handed manner. They believed these actions to be blasphemy. When he offended them by breaking the sabbath as they understood the sabbath, they were outraged because they were convinced that they knew what kind of behaviour pleased God.[44] Christ confronted religious leaders who had misinterpreted (perhaps it is better to say over-interpreted) the Law, and he showed them that they had misunderstood God's requirements. Christ did not enter a religious vacuum; thanks to the Old Testament his compatriots had a firm grasp of the existence of one sovereign God who loves salvation and justice.

Interpret me as though the Old Testament did not exist and you will have some kind of religion. It will certainly not be Christianity. Christianity is basically the belief that Jesus is Lord and that God raised him from the dead, but it is not only that. It is based on an already existing belief in a God who created everything out of nothing and revealed himself to a selected race of people.

Christianity is not merely a good idea that happened to be minted and gained currency around Jerusalem two thousand years ago; it is one stage in the continuing activity of a creative God. More particularly it is the repair stage. Mankind had run itself into confusion by disregarding the Manufacturer's instructions, and direct intervention by the Manufacturer was necessary. To make a good repair, certain painful measures were necessary. These measures had to prove painful for God or man. God chose the pain for himself. Jesus did the repair job and took the pain

58

upon himself. In doing so he established a new agreement between God and man which was a successor to the agreement made between God and Abraham.

Jesus was a Jew. So were the apostles. Luke managed to gain a place for himself in the annals of the new religion, and the Gospel he wrote sticks out like a sore thumb as a result. He had a concern for the welfare of women. He was a man of aesthetic sensibility. It was the urbane, polished and doubtless diplomatic physician who was able to escort Paul on his journeys when a more intransigent Jew like Barnabas found agreement impossible. Luke, who looked upon Galilee as a mere lake (where the Galilean peasants looked upon it as a sea), was the best possible person to chronicle the spread of a new religion from one end of the Mediterranean to the other, but it was not Luke who wrote the letters I contain. It was not Luke who meditated, wrestled with the problems of the growing Church, and interpreted the new religion in the light of the old. It was not Luke who made it plain that a second stage was now being ignited and that the first stage should now be allowed to fall away.

That task was reserved for St Paul and he did what Luke could never have done. St Paul had the Jewish faith in his bones. It was part of the essential man, not an ornament taken up like a Roman toga. Roman citizen he may have been, but Jew he was as much as Shylock. To fail to accept Paul's interpretation is to be content with half a Gospel. And half a Gospel is what you will have if you do without Paul's insistence on the Old Testament in making plain my message.

I'll tell you what you'll be missing.

You will not have the emphasis on law that puts the Gospel into its proper perspective. Much flabby sentimental Christianity has developed out of a lack of proper regard for the character of God and for the standards he expects from his creatures. Just as you can't have an easy relationship in a class-room unless the pupils clearly understand what level of behaviour their teacher expects and insists upon, so you cannot have a Father-son relationship between God and man unless there is the proper basis of respect—and, to use a particular Old Testament word, fear. The Gospel only comes into its own when a man or woman

59

realises the enormity of the shortcomings and transgressions he or she has committed or been party to.

Another thing that will be missing is God's insistence on justice in society. The Gospel shows love to be the supreme virtue, but love must be shaped and directed. To love indiscriminately is not the way to good government and fair dealing, and God expects both. The prophets made this plain. They were extremely interested in the nature of man's relationship with his fellows within an ordered society, and they called for changes in the order when it did not encourage right conduct.

Leave out the Old Testament and you will easily overlook the solidarity of the family unit and the responsibilities of parenthood. You may even find yourself being deceived into aiming to make Christians of children and young people behind their parents' backs.

I simply can't be interpreted as though I were self-sufficient. If you treat me like that, you're building a house without foundations. No, without the Old Testament I don't really make sense. I came to a prepared audience, and this determines the kind of book I am. Of course, I know that it is quite impracticable for your friends to be expected to do a long trudge through the Old Testament before they are allowed to open me. Their persistence would falter as they tried to cope with Leviticus or the history of the divided kingdom, and they would never reach me at all. You can't expect to repeat the historical process of educating the Jews to a pitch of readiness for my message. But what you *can* do is to look at the two of us together.

I have never pretended to be self-sufficient and I have no aspirations in that direction. So please do all you can to make sure that my friend and I are considered as the two-stage product we were meant to be. As often as not we are bound together in one volume—and if that doesn't underline the point I am trying to make I don't know what could do it better.

Chapter Seven

Nobody planned me

I say, it's strange how ready you human beings are to complain, don't you think? Perhaps it's not so strange though. I remember you complaining about the poor picture on your new television set and the adjustments that had to be made to the aerial. I back you to the hilt on complaints like that. Like you, I think it is important to get things *right*.

But I'm not thinking of that, really. I'm thinking of the way people complain about plays, poems and pictures. I'm thinking of the way they complain without attempting to understand the circumstances that gave rise to the play or whatever and helped to make it what it is.

You know very well that nothing is easier than to complain that a work of art is not as good as it ought to be, given the ability of the artist and his dedication to what he sees to be true. Nothing is easier, for example, than to condemn Shakespeare for including bawdry and violence in his plays. But a work of art must be understood in relation to the contemporary audience, not as an abstract exercise achieved by a hermit able to please himself and himself alone. Shakespeare had to write for the groundlings as well as for the patrons of the Mermaid tavern. Had he been too aloof to concern himself with popular taste you would not have had any plays at all. It was the audience that paid the gate-money when the flag went up at the theatres over the water, and it was the audience that made it possible for Shakespeare, having given the crowd what they wanted, to give them far more than they could have realised underneath the snap, crackle, pop.

But for the buffoons and the bloodshed you would not have had the most luminous poetry to grace the English stage. You would not have had delicate revelations of a man being corrupted by ambition, or jealousy, or self-doubt. You would not have had tender explorations of human love. That you have *Macbeth, Othello, Hamlet* and the rest at all is due to the crowds who applauded Kyd as well as Shakespeare. It was their patronage that made it all possible.

I admit that the parallel is not a precise one, but in a way what is true of Shakespeare is true of me. The letters of St Paul were the result of strife and confusion in the early Church. What the muddled and conceited believers drew from Paul was a collection of prime documents on the true meaning of the Gospel. Like Shakespeare's audiences, the members of the early Church got more than they bargained for. In both cases later generations benefited as much as those for whom the writing was originally done.

Doubtless, while Paul dictated, a messenger was pacing impatiently up and down outside the door, anxious not to miss the tide. The letters that came from Paul—and these are the first documents you have on the new religion (Christianity, as you now call it)—were probably written with one eye on whatever passed for a clock in those days.

You may be sure that Paul's writing rarely took place in a secluded library with ready access to reference books; it was an immediate response to a rapidly changing (sometimes worsening) situation. Should believing women separate from unbelieving husbands? Should believers eat meat which had been offered to idols at the time of slaughter? What was to be done about a believer who had run off with his stepmother? How far should church services be allowed to get mixed up with riotous dinners? Should impromptu sermons be allowed? Some of the questions with which Paul dealt are still pressing; others have scarcely any importance. The selection of letters that remain today is tantalising; most of my readers would like to know more about the row between Peter and Paul as recorded in Galatians two. Most would like to know what else Paul wrote to the believers in Corinth. But you and the other readers do not know and most probably never will know. You have to be content with the selection of documents that has survived.

By comparison with the epistles, the Gospels are leisurely products, and even—in the case of Luke's Gospel, particularly—carefully and stylishly composed. But the Gospels are vulnerable to academic criticism. As biographies they are unbalanced; they suggest insufficient research into the early life of Jesus. Had a present-day biographer turned in a manuscript like one of the Gospels he would have been sent away from his publisher with a flea in his ear; indeed, he would probably not have found any publisher at all prepared to accept his manuscript.

But, as I said right at the beginning, it is a matter of knowing what a thing is before you can decide on its worth. The Gospel-writers were writing for a particular audience—men and women who believed that Jesus was Lord (or were half-way to belief) and wanted to have in black and white some authentic stories about him. It was his public life they were interested in—what he said to people and how he affected their lives. The Gospels preserve the sayings and the incidents that brought them forth; it was sayings, incidents, miracles and the story of Jesus' death and resurrection that the first believers needed in written form, and in the shaping of the Gospels you can see something of the needs of the early Church. The things that seemed less important to believers in the days when the Gospels were being composed were forgotten and left out.

You have to approach the epistles and Gospels, then, as documents coming into existence in the heat and ferment of the first generation of the new religion which came to be called—but not by me—Christianity. The documents bear all the marks of the pressures, quarrels, misunderstandings and triumphant confidence that went to make up the shape of the early Church. It is a mistake to study the documents as though they were articles solicited from distinguished experts for a new encyclopaedia. On the contrary, the documents have the qualities of uncalculating candour and honest effort that distinguish good plain journalism. They lack metaphysical wit and philosophical subtlety. Even the old man's Gospel, John, is characterised by musing rather than by epigram.

If you acknowledge the hand-to-mouth way in which I came into being, you will not complain about my lack of smoothness. I was not edited into one harmonious whole; I am a collection of hurried compositions still in their original form, not tied up or made presentable. Many people recognise that this enhances the authenticity of the collection even if it sometimes makes them think of a badly cut jig-saw or a school-child's essay which has not been looked over before it is handed in.

As with Shakespeare, the best way to understand the worth of my text is to compare it not with some vague ideal composition floating at the back of your mind but with the actual productions of contemporaries. In the case of Shakespeare this means a comparison with the plays of Jonson and Webster and the sonnets of Daniel and Drayton. In my case it means a comparison with the apocryphal gospels. I don't think it would be overweening pride on my part to say that men find the latter tedious and fantastic— if they have ever bothered to read them. My Gospels may be untidy, even scrappy, but they do not fall into sentimentality, and I think I can claim to be packed with incident and straight-forward vigorous writing.

Don't forget that the form in which you have the Gospels is largely attributable to piecemeal editorial work. Stories which were passed from one person to another by word of mouth were collected by the Gospel-editors into manuscripts and linked together in an order and with comments that seemed sensible and helpful. The Gospel-writers did not function so much as re-porters as sub-editors. They selected their material with a particular end in view. In the case of Mark the intention appears to have been to set down the actions of Jesus. In the case of Matthew the intention was to demonstrate the new faith as a development of the old. The Gospel of Luke was a more con-scious piece of authorship in which the particular sympathies of the writer determine the shape of the finished product. The fourth Gospel is the work of a man who saw himself in the role of interpreter rather than editor.

The Gospel-writers had to make what they could of the material that was available. I can imagine Luke, with his note-book in his hand, talking to strangers on their doorsteps. I can see him afterwards in a nearby inn writing up his notes by the light of an oil-lamp. Mark—well, I can imagine him sitting like a shorthand typist while Peter struggled to dictate his reminiscences. As for Matthew, I can picture him rummaging through the Old Testament, making notes, and setting out to demonstrate that the new religion is the fulfilment of the old. I'm not claiming, of course, that my contributors were the first men to put stories of Jesus down in black and white; I just don't know.

One thing I am fairly clear about: the Gospel-writers did not have a team of research assistants ferreting out information, checking facts, testing sources. By present-day standards they probably worked with minimum equipment. They did have a large amount of goodwill (every believer was probably anxious to contribute what he could to the production—if he knew about it) and there was a network to put the various men and women concerned in touch with one another, but in general the writers had to do the best they could with what they could find.

As far as the epistles are concerned, you have what are often occasional writings, writings designed, that is, to meet particular, urgent needs. For the Roman Christians, Paul set down at some length the general shape of the new faith, and for the Ephesian believers (if it was for Ephesians that Paul was writing) Paul wrote in similar general terms. But for the benefit of the turbulent Corinthians Paul raced to utter warnings before his readers, like hot-headed children, did some serious damage to themselves and to the cause which had aroused their enthusiasm. Seeing the Galatians about to embark on a foolhardy venture which would have jeopardised the new faith throughout the world, Paul wrote urgently (and at one point you might say almost indecently) to restrain them from their folly. To the Thessalonian believers Paul sent letters designed to quench their thirst for rash speculation about the Second Coming of Christ.

Much of Shakespeare's dramatic poetry can be understood only in the light of the conditions prevailing in the Elizabethan theatre. The soliloquies of Richard the Third, for example, are more immediately intelligible in dramatic terms if they are seen as coming from an actor standing virtually among the audience and confiding in them. Paul's vigorous (and occasionally immoderate) terms are best understood if he is recognised as one who is plunged into the whirl of life in all the churches.

I don't want to apologise for myself; at the same time I don't want you to get wrong ideas about me. To repeat a point I made earlier, I was never edited as a whole. Some parts of me were more carefully pruned and polished than others. Some parts are manifestly assembled with the care and skill lavished by an author with all the time in the world, or by a technologist working on a space project. Other parts of me have the tang of immediacy, like personal letters never designed to be read by any other eyes than those of the addressee. It has always to be remembered, therefore, that a distinctive vocabulary ("immediately" in Mark, for example) and distinctive categories (the fulfilment of tabernacle ritual in Hebrews) are employed by different writers; there is no semblance of uniformity.

Perhaps the rush and fury of organising the churches left no time for considered writing and editing. Perhaps it never occurred to the writers that they were turning out documents that people like you would be studying closely nineteen centuries later. There was certainly nothing like a New Testament conference to decide how the finished product should be balanced. More editorial planning goes into a Sunday paper than went into me.

The man who bears in mind the pressures and needs that shaped me will better understand my message for today than the man who reads it as a uniform piece of writing dictated by God to a number of men who could have been interchanged without anybody noticing the difference. Because I am a collection of living documents I must always be looked at against my background—and sometimes you will not know enough about that to come to any final conclusion. As far as interpreting goes, you must be ready to live and let live.

With all this said, my opinion is that I gain rather than lose by being a casual production rather than an elaborately ordered set-piece. And remember: the fact that I am a miscellaneous collection of items without the unity that you find in a well constructed play is no disqualification of my claim to be a document of the highest importance. I notice that much of your modern drama is a reaction—and a fruitful reaction—against the well constructed, naturalistic play. What I think you humans call the "epic" theatre is a matter of loosely connected scenes rather than a tight-knit development. What you call the "alienation" effect is another example of what at first appears to be dramatic untidiness. I am quite happy therefore for people in your generation to be expected to take me as I am and to find me full of ambiguities, puzzles and disturbing ideas.

But more than this, I believe that my coming into being had a kind of inevitability about it. I was not carefully planned and composed by men organising a new religion. They did what they did under the compulsion of God. They were moved by the Holy Spirit to set down what they did in black and white. They were— to use a word which is easily misunderstood—inspired. The result is that the form which I finally assumed is precisely the form God wanted me to have. Behind the lack of conscious planning and editorial work is the creative activity of God, of God speaking to men and women in all subsequent generations. What you have is the result not of superficial planning but of the kind of deep mastering urge that results in men putting into words more than they realise. So don't be misled by what looks like superficial scrappiness. The kind of planning involved in my production was too profound to be left to the conscious decisions of my writers.

If I were you, I shouldn't worry too much about this aspect. It will make itself plain enough as you read me with an alert mind. I'm more concerned to get over to you the kind of production I am. If you remember the way in which I came into being, it will help you to retain a sense of proportion. You will not expect local churches today to be devoid of argument and clashing opinions; had the clash and argument been absent from the early Church, a considerable part of me would never have been written. Nor will you expect a simple solution to the problems facing the Church at the present time. You will rather expect to encounter the same pitfalls and painful experiences as your New Testament forebears, and you will not be discouraged if the Church to which you belong seems sometimes to be only too human, too quarrelsome, too worldly.

There, that's how I came to be what I am. Don't be misled by my elegant binding!

Chapter Eight

Pets – what are they?

Oh yes, there's one thing I'm glad about; you don't camouflage me.

Yes, camouflage. *Camouflage.* What I mean is that, unlike a good many others, you don't stick to the Authorised Version. Often I'm so much camouflaged in obsolescent English— "musick", "savourest" and all that—that people can hardly understand me at all. People forget that over a period of 300 years the spoken and written language steadily moved further and further away from the language used by the wisest fool in Christendom. My best friend in recent years has been J. B. Phillips. He tore off the camouflage in no uncertain fashion.

It can happen to any literature, of course. Any book is dust and ashes if it is locked up in obsolete forms—as the English teacher found when she introduced Nevil Coghill's translation of *The Canterbury Tales* into the school. A parent who had complacently smiled upon his child's efforts to make sense of Chaucer in the original was moved to a storm of fury and a trip to the school by reading in modern English what Chaucer had written in Middle English.

But in my case it is not just a matter of a contemporary translation. My true meaning can equally well be hidden by confining my application to a nineteenth-century situation.

To interpret my message for a nineteenth-century labouring man tempted to chronic drunkenness (as an escape from the intolerable conditions which others had permitted to surround him) is a different matter from interpreting it for a twentieth-century family man with leisure-time interests beyond the wildest dreams of his grandfather. Indeed, the better the message is interpreted for the drunken labourer, the less meaningful it may be to the computer programmer. Every generation must have the message interpreted afresh. But it's not easy.

I admit that in some respects I myself am to blame. I came into a world of camels and sheep-folds and here you are in a world of computers and jet-planes. I can scarcely blame you if I am occasionally misunderstood for that reason. In some respects I might as well be a visitor from another planet. A camel was the biggest animal people knew in my day; today you can see an elephant or a giraffe in any zoo, and your Michael, I know, is quite at home amongst the dinosaurs, so in some ways I am bound to appear a little provincial. When you consider, too, that a vineyard was the most highly-organised industrial unit in my world, you are bound to think me a little pedestrian.

Of course, the plain truth of the matter is that I can't teach you anything about how to answer technical questions—and I'm afraid you have more and more technical questions to answer these days. But the really important questions remain, and all your technical expertise won't solve them—questions like: What is man? Is there a meaning in life? Is love the supreme virtue? It's questions like these that I'm really interested in but I don't talk about them in everyday, familiar terms which would be immediately meaningful to your contemporaries.

What I'm waiting for is somebody who will turn my stories about sheep and shepherds, slaves and masters, yokes and ploughs, into stories about production-lines and advertising agencies. It might seem presumptuous to transpose my contents in this way, but if this isn't done, I can see myself becoming a forgotten book in another generation.

Another thing—animals. Now, what animals have you got about the house? A Labrador, a hamster and a goldfish. Quite. As I thought, they're all pets. You won't find pets on my pages, The only animals I know are wild animals, working animals and edible animals. The animals my writers knew are completely different from the animals you know—or, to put it another way,

74

your relationship with animals is quite different from the relationship men of my day had with animals.

Now, if this is the case, why don't you get one of your friends to turn my animal stories into stories about the animals *you* know? I once saw this done in the *Church of England Newspaper*. The result was as follows: "God is my master; I shall never be short of food or exercise. My master gives me red meat every day and keeps my water-bowl full. My master takes me for good long walks and looks after me when I am ill. Even when I am down in the dumps, I know that he will still pick up the lead and whistle me to join him. Happy is the animal that lives in a dog-house like mine."

It's not only a matter of sheep and the twenty-third psalm. Your friends would more readily get the point if you substituted "elephant" for "camel" and said that it was harder for a rich man to enter the kingdom of God than for an elephant to go through the eye of a needle. Sunflowers are more familiar than mustard plants, so why not say that the kingdom of heaven is like a sunflower seed which, tiny as it is, produces a monster of a plant eight feet high with flowers like dinner plates? Instead of referring to a man with a mill-stone round his neck, why not refer to a man with a couple of old car batteries round his neck?

If anybody says that to treat me like this is sacrilege, I can only say that no treatment is worse than being praised on all hands but never read. My most uncomfortable moments come when I am collecting dust on a shelf alongside the complete works of Shakespeare and Charles Dickens. I get stiff, bored and frustrated. I might just as well be last year's gonk or A Present from Littlehampton.

If you are going to transpose me like this, you have got to be sure you are getting on to the wavelength of the people for whose benefit you are transposing. Let me see. What is the most popular daily paper in the country? The *Daily Mirror*? And what are the subjects that interest its readers most?

I see. Well, if people are interested in royalty, animals and people, you must start with royalty, animals and people—and probably, if I may add a suggestion, a bit of football thrown in.

What's that? You think that my language and interests are

nearer those of the *Daily Mirror* than they are near the language and interests of learned theologians? Ah, yes. I'm interested you should say that. I want to say something later on about what the theologians have done to me. But for the moment let me say this: whatever you think of the Gospels, you cannot deny that they are warm, earthy and human. They are not abstract and remote.

I can't think why preachers so often make me seem so dull. As far as I can tell, I am not a dull book, but I notice that when a man stands in the pulpit to explain me, everybody looks sleepy. Don't they give your preachers the kind of training that a good sub-editor gets? Don't they teach preachers how to make things interesting?

One of the big mistakes people make about me is to think that I am just interested in religion. This infuriates me. My writers have got something to say on all the big decisions of life. To upgrade religion to the status of a special department appears to be very enlightened, but in fact it all too often means that my message is trivialised; it becomes a matter of meetings in the church hall and spare-time activities. It also results in my being confined to ecclesiastical proprietorship; men and women outside the Church think I have nothing to say to *them*.

What you and your friends need is a determination to "connect", as E. M. Forster would say. It is all very well for my revelation to be available in book form, but if it stays in the book it is doing no good to anybody. I and the people who need me must be put in touch with one another. The problem must be tackled from the two ends—the scholars must examine the meaning of my text and elucidate it as far as they can, and people like you must raise the questions that confront responsible people living in the world today. The man in the middle who tries to keep in touch with both groups must be something of a prophet. Like most men in the middle, he will have an uncomfortable time, but nothing less than this kind of job will enable me to make an impact on the minds of men today.

In the Middle Ages the Church faced the same problem. It was failing to get its message across. People were bored with the same old services and the same old sermons. So something new was tried—drama. Quite accidentally the Church brought to light a forgotten art form. At first it was very unambitious. Two or three priests enacted incidents from the Gospels. First the drama took place in the church, then outside. As you know, the drama got out of hand. King Herod and Noah's wife soon assumed an importance not sanctioned by the text and not particularly helpful to the story. The whole thing developed into something the Church could not control. But doubtless the Church was right to take the risk in the first place, just as it was right for St Francis to found his order of friars and for William Booth to found the Salvation Army. Christianity is a risk-taking religion and has been from the start. You have to ask yourselves today whether you are not playing unduly for safety, whether your caution and respect for decorum are not muffling my message.

It's not enough, though, as I was saying, to put me into modern terms, to transpose me from a world of sheep, shepherds, bushels and fishing-nets into a world of jet-planes, ball-points, customs barriers and copying-machines. It could mean no more than putting *Dick Whittington* on ice or putting *Hamlet* into modern dress. What you must do is to show that my fundamental message is still relevant today. And that is a much harder job.

Part of the trouble is that people today are so contented. They have come into possession of everyday benefits that two or three generations ago would have been restricted to aristocrats and newly-rich industrialists. They are like children with new toys. You can scarcely blame them for being a bit excited about it all. In the middle of all this hubbub, with something "new" coming out every day, it's not surprising if I look a little flat and faded. Like poetry, I have gone down in popular estimation.

If you are going to persuade people to take me seriously nowadays, you have got a big job in hand. You must reintroduce people to a whole range of things that they have overlooked—and serious literature is part of that range. That is why education is such a crucial matter for you believers. You can't reintroduce a generation to serious literature in five minutes; it's a question of a child's entire school career and more. If a boy or a girl cannot appreciate what good things there are in Conan Doyle's *The Lost World* or Robert Bolt's *A Man for All Seasons*, it is unlikely that they will be able to come to terms with more demanding literature—like me, for instance. So, as More says to Rich in Robert Bolt's play, my advice to an enthusiastic young man or woman in Christ would be, "Be a teacher". A teacher can introduce me to young people in the context of other books and a lively community where I can show my paces in a convincing way.

Some people, of course, have missed that chance. They have gone through their school-days without ever coming into contact with me in any meaningful way. I am a closed book to them. And I think you will have to conclude regretfully that I am likely to remain a closed book. If you can't train and encourage a child to know God from the start, I'm afraid you won't have too much success with a crash-course laid on for him in adult life. At least, this is how it seems to the Old Testament and me. Being a disciple of Christ is a lifelong study and if you miss the preliminary lessons (which in my time meant being a Jew, or a synagogue-inquirer) you are handicapped for the rest of your life. Occasionally you get the startling conversion of a man who has never been in touch with Christianity before, but it is rash to draw conclusions from an event like that.

The other thing that must be done is to argue from the principles you find in me to the situations and problems confronting people today. This is not done nearly enough; my message is allowed to determine belief and individual behaviour but little more. In fact the Old Testament and I have far wider interests—as you would discover if you started from the problems before you and asked what I have to say about them.

Of course, I don't specifically talk about four-day working weeks and comprehensive schools and export drives, but I think you will find that there is an extraordinary similarity between efficient management methods and parts of the Sermon on the Mount. The principles have been there all the time for those who care to read them and apply them to prevailing conditions (that is where your technical expertise comes in), but in the rough and tumble of human activity they often get overlooked.

Again, do you remember that little story about counting the cost?[45] Jesus said that a king planning to go to war would, if he were sensible, ask himself whether the odds were favourable. If they weren't, he would sue for peace terms before he was catastrophically defeated. Now in the first instance that story shows that you must count the cost before becoming a follower of Christ, but the story has other implications. What Jesus is urging men to do in this story is to ask: "What is the alternative?" And this is the question that the realist asks. He wants to know what other possible courses of action there are before he commits himself to a course of action that seems gravely impracticable.

By appealing to men's common sense in a matter like this, Jesus was dealing in the terms in which day-to-day decisions are made. A man building a tower, a king going to war, and a woman planning her household budget must all decide on priorities. If they want to buy one thing, they must go without another. If they spend money one day, they cannot spend it the next. If they use up their savings on something they cannot afford to maintain, they are inviting trouble. By setting the matter of becoming a disciple against these unforgiving daily choices Jesus was compelling his hearers to take realistic decisions. He was not encouraging them to enjoy flights of idealism and religious sentiment. He was demanding practical choices.

Now practical choices often require you human beings to select the lesser of two evils. In the matter, for instance, of making contraceptives available to unmarried people, the practical choice is between a society in which there is promiscuous sexual intercourse followed by illegitimate babies and a society in which there is promiscuous sexual intercourse not followed by illegitimate babies. These are the only two choices available. To duck the question—to say, for example, that you should not accept anything less than Gospel morality in your country today—is to bury your head in the sand.

You believers need to do much more to show that you are practical in this kind of way about the decisions that have to be made in society today. You have to be prepared to make a thorough job of something that is no better than the lesser of two evils. It is no good pining for ideal solutions or a world full of men and women who are obedient to the Gospel; you have to accept what you have been given and live in the world in which you were born. (You also have to recognise that a baptized man can as easily be a muddler as the next man and in a position of responsibility a muddling Christian can do just as much damage as a muddling non-Christian.) I can't make it easy for you and I can't do your thinking for you either, but I can say that if you take me seriously in whatever circumstances you find yourself, and if you exercise your special knowledge and skills in the light of my message, you won't be entirely without a sense of direction. And people with a sense of direction get noticed in your topsy-turvy world today.

Chapter Nine

I can't be responsible for men's opinions

I've had something on my mind since our last conversation. I'm a bit worried in case I have given you the impression that once you have turned my stories about sheep and shepherds into stories about jet-planes and customs-barriers, and once you have shown that what I have to say is important to your contemporaries, all your troubles are over.

That's far from the truth, of course. I can't command men's opinions. If you make my message as clear and convincing as a motorway sign, there is no guarantee that men will take any notice of it. Some will; some won't. It's very similar to human behaviour on a motorway; with the clearest information about road conditions at their disposal, some drivers will ignore the hazards and drive in such a way as to risk their own lives and the lives of other people. They put their own early arrival (or hopes of it) above appropriate safety measures. They know what they ought to do, but they decide to do something else. Or perhaps they don't do any deciding at all; they just do what they always do; they are creatures of habit.

I realise that to regard human beings in this way is distinctly unflattering. But I am afraid that in this respect I am a distinctly unflattering book. One of the things I am always emphasising is the fact that men need outside help if they are to avoid destruction. As you know, I use words like "grace", "election" and "regeneration" to make this point plain. Once you begin to consider the human predicament at all seriously, you find that this emphasis answers to something deep about human nature. I should be tampering with the truth if I gave you the impression that things were otherwise.

Think of the way you human beings ignore manufacturers' instructions. Not always, of course. You know very well what happens if you make a wrong connection when you fit a plug to the cable of an electric heater, or if you put the wrong grade of petrol into the tank of your Rover. People aren't often careless about things like that; they think too much of themselves (their mortal selves, that is) and their cars. I'm sure that other examples of men ignoring manufacturers' instructions will readily come to your mind. . . .

What was that? Oh, yes—winding on films, cleaning gramophone records and gutters, mixing weed-killer in the right proportions, keeping tyres at the right pressure. All right! That's enough! You see my point: nothing is more common than to find men ignoring instructions, no matter how well they may know them.

You human beings, in fact, are not calm, rational creatures who choose to do what is right and best after weighing up the issues. You are betrayed by self-interest, laziness and bad habits. You share willy-nilly in the confusion, muddle and waste that seem to dominate the human scene; even when you know what you ought to do, you fail to do it.

This is one of the curious aspects of human nature. You do what you think fit regardless of what other, wiser people may have to say on the matter. You all think you know best. I could be shouting my head off to warn people, but it would do no good at all. When men are bent on destruction, they will hurtle along the road to it despite any warnings they may be given.

Think of the passion and vehemence with which Paul addressed Jews and Gentiles and warned members of the early Church about dangers ahead. You might have thought it would be impossible to ignore his blazing urgency and his torrential pleas. Not a bit of it! Some chose to shut their ears to his Gospel. His pleading was almost entirely in vain in Athens, for example.[46]

The same happens today. There are still believers who show

apostolic enthusiasm (not to mention imagination and cunning) in attempting to divert their fellow human beings from unbelief and contempt of God. The believers make unceasing efforts to put the Gospel message convincingly and winningly before their neighbours, but the message is ignored. Men know that Christ died so that they might be forgiven and restored; they know that their proper response is to turn from their own way and go God's way; but they choose not to do so.

It's all down in my pages—at some length in St Paul's letter to the Romans. And this is a level at which all the changing of sheep into household pets is not going to achieve anything at all. For this is going deeper than getting something across. This is a matter of recognising and exposing something that is wrong with human beings deep down.

Probably it's foolish to expect ordinary people to study Romans (and Hebrews, too, for that matter) at all closely. Probably you have to recognise that these letters are just not suitable for people brought up in this bustling world of yours. Most of you would do better—if you are going to read me at all—to concentrate on the shorter, the more manageable bits, the parables and Gospel-stories. You'll just have to admit that some parts of me are not suitable for general reading in a generation that only reads the easy stuff.

However, whether people read Romans or whether they don't, the fact remains that understanding my message is not everything. What is important is whether my message is accepted and obeyed deep down in a man. At the end of the day this is the thing that really counts.

Accepted—that's the point. When I said earlier on that the teaching material of Jesus has a good deal in common with the content of the *Daily Mirror*, I was not suggesting that both are equally *acceptable*. Obviously it is far less demanding to read a new edition of the *Daily Mirror* every day than to struggle to extract the meaning from some of those problematic parables which have teased men's minds since they were first composed. (And you don't find anything like Romans in a popular paper.)

No, what is common to both the *Mirror* and the Gospels is warmth and humanity—and it is important that you believers should see the force of this when you set out to approach your contemporaries. You have got to start at the right place if you want to gain their attention and take them along with you. But you must also recognise that what is not common to the *Mirror* and the Gospels is the uncompromising nature of the Gospel message. It does not go half-way to meet its audience; however interestingly it may be presented, it tells its audience quite bluntly that it is time they submitted to their Creator.

Of course, your generation has brought to a fine art the matter of giving the customer what he requires. That market research interviewer who called a few days ago makes that plain. Even old-fashioned British motor-car manufacturers are now beginning to take pains to find out what sort of car a driver actually wants before they design a new model. Engineers are horrified; what they are interested in, after all, is good engineering, as advanced as possible. But if the customer wants a spurious sportiness allied with unadventurous engineering, that's what the designers will aim at, and that is what the engineers will have to provide.

In your society the consumer sets the pace. The man who pays the piper has always called the tune, but he can call it more effectively these days when consumers are marshalled in their millions. Every consumer expects to be wooed, therefore, to have his whims indulged and his lightest fancy heeded. The dream tends to crumple, of course, when it comes to service and maintenance, but for the man about to purchase a consumer durable (as I believe you call a big item of domestic equipment), the world is at his feet. Or if it is not actually at his feet, it is made to appear so by a go-getting salesman.

Myself, I don't set out to please consumers. I'm not a book that adapts itself to the whims and fancies of mankind. My essential message is not modified to suit each generation. And this, I suppose, is unforgivable in the eyes of your contemporaries. If motor-cars and refrigerators and electric heaters can be designed according to customers' requirements, why cannot different brands of religion be available?

It sounds reasonable, and in a sense I support the idea of different brands—different versions of the Way of Christ, that is.

I do not expect all believers to take the same view of everything. It would be as dull for me as for you if believers all went away from me with a set of identical reach-me-down opinions that were one hundred per cent predictable. But as far as the essentials are concerned, I can't make any compromise at all. I can't go half-way, even one-sixteenth way, to meet the opinion of unbelievers. I have no discretion whatever to modify my message so as to make it acceptable to potential believers. They have to take my message as it is.

What my writers put at the centre of their message is, in fact, something which seems quite *un*acceptable, the death of Jesus Christ on a cross. It is when men identify themselves with this, when they enter into Christ, when they accept the need for a kind of death and resurrection as *he* died and rose, that the message takes effect.

It is the invitation to men to do this that makes me unique among the world's books. Plato may have invited men to put themselves into the hands of guardians who would look after their interests and order society for their well-being, but *I* invite men to undergo a kind of voluntary death and to become new men. Nobody could mistake this for a programme designed to win favourable reactions all round. It might well be thought to be designed with the opposite end in view.

Don't think I'm merely being arrogant when I talk about my message in a take-it-or-leave-it way. It is just beyond my power to trim my message for the benefit of your generation or any other generation. I am one place where the consumer must learn to accept what he is given. And "given" is the word, because the potential believer is not paying for this message and has no ground for expecting alterations.

I'm well aware that my message has to be presented differently in different circumstances. Children obviously need a different presentation from the presentation needed by university dons. But whatever efforts are made to present my message in clear, even popular, terms, the toughness remains; it can be eliminated only by turning my message into something else altogether.

To some extent the toughness *has* been eliminated, I'm afraid. There have been men in all generations who have preferred to see me soft and flabby. It's disgusting! When I think what it was like in the beginning. . . .

In my day, getting my message across meant an unending struggle. In the course of the struggle my writers and their friends were often run out of town, beaten up and thrown into prison. An eye-witness of those days would never have believed it possible that the new religion could prove to be dull or un-noticeable—any more than an eye-witness of the days of Danton, Robespierre and the rest would have believed that the French Revolution could turn into quiet, respectable republicanism.

But the impossible has happened. People read from me in great, beautiful buildings and in cosy groups by the fireside. I feel I have been tamed. I am allowed to say my piece, but not to disturb the prevailing patterns of church life. If I am saying that the Church as a whole must fall into the ground like a seed and die in order to send up new shoots, this message is not heard. Members of the Church are content with notionally omnicompetent ministers, mute and apathetic lay people, patriarchal leadership, dioceses, missionary societies, theological colleges, church magazines, Christmas, Lent, robes, prayer books, patronage, churchwardens and churchyards, when I know nothing of these. I'm not saying these things are wrong; I am only asking whether you and your friends have considered the possibility that there might be better ways of doing things.

Do you see what I'm driving at? Often the very people who read me most and could be expected to understand me most clearly are much more conditioned by prevailing modes than by obedience to my requirements. All too often those who make the strongest professions of allegiance to me are the most inflexible and hidebound. Inside the Church the position all too often is that I am understood but I am not allowed to determine policy. It is almost as though I am muzzled. And if that can happen inside the Church is it surprising that I am not making much impression outside?

Chapter Ten

Don't hand me over to the experts

A word in your ear!

Do you know the best way to jeopardise what you call Christianity?

Exactly. Destroy every copy of me that exists.

And the next best way is to hand me over lock, stock and barrel to the experts.

Believers are so ready to do this themselves that enemies of the Gospel need hardly do more than arrange for a little discreet encouragement to be provided. A few bland words about the original Greek or the Aramaic behind this or that verse and the layman retires baffled. He begins to have a feeling that I am not intended for his private reading, that the perils facing the un-witting reader are so great that the task is better not essayed.

I can well understand how such a man must feel. Nobody likes to look a fool when the carefully nurtured opinions of years are demolished in a few moments by a bright young New Testament scholar, so the prudent course seems to be to make a humble confession of ignorance and wait for the experts to make their pronouncements. If you disagree with what they say, you can, if you are patient enough, be sure to find other experts who will say something more congenial to you.

This handing me over to the experts is something that you must avoid at all costs. For one thing they pull me about merci-lessly. Sometimes I end up altogether re-arranged, back to front, inside-out, so that my own writers would not recognise me. It's excruciatingly painful. I feel quite ill at the thought of it. . . .

But that's my worry, not yours. I mustn't bother you with my troubles. In any case, some of the theologians are very gentle. They treat me with—I was going to say reverence. Their one concern is to find out what I am really saying. I feel safe in their hands.

However, to return to our subject: you believers should not hand me over to the experts, because when you do that you establish a rank of intermediaries between God and man. Let the experts tell you what they have discovered, let them write their books, but don't expect them to do your thinking for you, and don't imagine that I was written merely to keep scholars busy in their studies. Shakespeare's plays, remember, were written to be performed; so—in a different sense—was I.

If I am taken into the study, I should be taken there as a racing-car might be taken into a workshop—to be investigated by experts. Just as a racing-car has to come out of the workshop and justify itself by its performance on the track, so I have to justify myself by my effect on the Church. I am not a book for academic study—like Malory's *Morte d'Arthur*; I'm a book to be taken into the thick of things.

Remember this. However good they are, experts develop interests of their own. The scholar amongst his books has lectures to prepare, students' work to criticise, research to do. His responsibilities are of a different kind from those borne by people in everyday occupations. The pace of intellectual life around him is quicker than that of most of you, and he is less concerned with the mundane tasks involved in keeping the world going each day. He is not daily obliged to accommodate himself to the pace of those who are appreciably slower than he is. In fact scholars often have more in common with other scholars than with people in everyday occupations who share their convictions. What I offer is a way of life to be lived by people of all abilities and backgrounds; it is important that all those who are following my way should be helping others along it, making discoveries as they go and learning from each other. This can only be done if I am a shared book which all are endeavouring to understand and obey.

The experts in question may be not so much academic theologians as leaders with strong personalities. If a leader has laid down a strong line about having no truck with interests that he thinks to be dangerous for believers, a strong conformist party tends to form. It is always easier to follow a path cut by somebody else than to carve your own path, and the baptized man is often as lazy as the next man. Before long the leader's prohibitions are accepted as humbly and obediently as the New Testament message itself; men of independent mind who take a different view then take on the appearance of fighting against the truth.

The danger is particularly marked in a form of religion with a strong authoritarian emphasis. The authority of God, or of God's Word, tends to be attributed to particular interpretations of the Word. The leader collects an authority greater than that which would be conceded to him in other departments of life because he seems to occupy a prophet's position.

Of course, the benefits of deference to leaders of this kind are not trifling. Cohesion is the most obvious. A body of believers united behind a small group of leaders—even if the believers do not quite know why they are behind them—is a formidable phalanx. Mutual support and encouragement increase the cohesiveness. The group grows strong as its members confirm one another's views and frown on deviations. But the price to be paid is high. Deference to experts does not make for initiative and responsibility; it rather fosters an inert, passive type of personality that waits for orders instead of making a personal judgement. It also encourages the evils as well as the strength of group thinking—a censorious outlook, small-mindedness, intolerance and smugness. I don't find these characteristics very attractive myself and I'm sure you don't either.

No. If Jesus was against anything, he was against the monopolising of religion by the professionals. His slighting remarks on their influence earned their detestation, and brought about a conspiracy to overthrow him. The whole weight of his teaching favoured an independent assessment and a personal decision rather than a period of waiting to see what the pundits might say. Of course, theology (which is, or should be, right thinking about God) is essential, but it must be kept in its place. Experts make maps by which others plan their journeys; the travellers do not leave all the travelling to the map-makers. Experts make dictionaries to which poets may refer; the poets do not leave the making of poetry to the lexicographers. Theological experts chart the outlines of revelation; it is rank and file believers who must shape an expression of the revelation in their daily decisions and activities.

It has to be remembered, too, that my pages concern themselves not only with theological matters, such as the redemptive work of Christ. The teaching of Jesus concerned itself with men's attitude to their enemies, with the hollowness of outward show, with the merit of single-mindedness and persistence, with the need for a trusting and generous spirit, with the meaning of a full life. Whether you are a Christian or not, these are important matters, and it is right and proper to give attention to what one of the significant books in the history of the world (for so I regard myself) has to say about them.

Put me on the kitchen table rather than on the scholar's desk any day. I was designed for a popular audience. Jesus' ministry was directed to a popular audience. Paul meant his letters (or some of them, at any rate) to be read out to groups of believers. In its early days what you call Christianity was a popular religion—and by "popular" I mean, of course, that it struck a chord among common people. Occasionally you would find a tycoon like Barnabas in the Church, but for the most part the new movement prospered among slaves and women—to the disgust of some of the Hellenistic believers, who expected it to develop into something much more intellectual and exclusive.

When I ask you not to deliver me into the hands of the experts, there are one or two exceptions I must make. I am always content to be in the hands of a prophet, because a prophet is a man with his feet on the ground and a real understanding of the life of the people around him. He keeps his eyes open and sees things as they actually are. He sees the truth of things. He is not prepared to accept the customary interpretation. Like the novelist or the poet who looks for the truth of the matter, he sees things uncomfortably clearly and describes them compellingly. He also goes on to express a verdict by applying my message to what he has seen. This is the way I like to be handled. I feel it's

94

what I'm made for. It's exhausting but I can see things happening as a result. I know you can't organise this kind of thing, but I find myself longing for prophets to show themselves today.

Sometimes there are clergymen who do this prophetic job well. They open me up and give down-to-earth advice to people facing practical problems. They don't talk in vague terms as though reading me and saying set prayers is the way to solve any problem; they apply me to the situation as thoroughly and honestly as they can. This is when I really come into my own. I can think of many people who have seen which way to go and have been nerved to take the right decision because of a clergyman doing his job in this way. But often clergymen are not encouraged to do this kind of job because people like you will not insist on putting practical questions to them. Clergymen need a flow of questions and comments from fellow-believers so that they know what is going on in the minds of those whom they are serving. It depends on you to a *very* large extent.

Of course, some clergymen get things back to front. They think lay people are there to help *them*. So instead of helping lay people to fulfil their responsibilities as parents, citizens, employees, etc., they look upon lay people as supporters and organisers of church organisations, as helpers of the clergy, in fact. This completely thwarts me. I end up being minutely discussed in inward-looking groups and totally ignored in the world at large. Can you imagine any position more embarrassing for a book like me?

Chapter Eleven

No imagination!

No imagination, that's the trouble, no imagination!

Oh, hullo! I didn't know you were there. I was just making some notes for you.

Do you know, there was a time when I never thought you would pay any attention to my notes, and here we are so far advanced that I haven't got anything ready to say to you.

What's that? You thought you heard something about imagination? You were right. I was just saying that some people have no imagination.

Yes, I thought you would agree. . . . Yes, I do think that that new housing-estate is very dull—and the interior decorating of that church you sometimes take me to—ugh! What a painful experience it can be! You know, I sometimes think that, with all its technology, your generation is the most unimaginative there has been since the world began. Facts, facts, facts! Sometimes I think people must come to Henry Reed's *Naming of Parts* for facts and information. Perhaps there are people who go to a football ground to count the blades of grass on the field. No imagination!

Some people, of course, suspect the imagination. It may be that they are members of a government or a bureaucracy and they don't like plays and stories that poke fun at them. After all, there's nothing like an *Animal Farm* to deflate people who take themselves over-seriously. The beauty of that kind of approach is that it cuts the ground from under the feet of the pompous ones. They're quite accustomed to hearing themselves and their policies discussed seriously; that kind of criticism can be countered by arguments and denials—and possibly statistics. But when you've slipped on a banana skin put there by somebody else, you've lost your dignity. Everybody's so busy laughing that anything you have to say just isn't heard.

Again, other people despise the imagination. They look upon it as a bit of embroidery round the edges of the human brain, as a source of fanciful ideas, but of no more importance in everyday life than the copper ornaments round the fireplace. I could weep to see middle-aged people who think that way. Once they were children living a rich life amongst their toys, sensitive to all the impressions around them, acute perceptive beings. Now they have become inert. They see and hear everything through a kind of filter; indeed, in severe cases they hardly see and hear at all. I often think that one of the most profound things that Jesus said was: "He that hath ears to hear, let him hear." One of the most important things you human beings have to do is to keep your eyes and ears open as you grow from childhood to manhood.

Think how readily children take to poetry. They ride from Ghent to Aix, they travel on Auden's *Night Mail*, they soar with Tennyson's *Eagle*. In one week at school they may fly higher and travel farther than their parents ever do. In their reading of poems they are penetrating into the stuff of life; they are experiencing things richly, whereas their parents are only skimming over the surface of them. Something of this capacity for seeing, hearing and feeling must have been in Jesus' mind when he put a child into the middle of his friends and told them that they must become like this if they wanted to know the secrets of the kingdom of heaven.

As children grow up, however, they become preoccupied. They forget to keep their eyes open. They cease to create stories and to identify themselves with heroes and villains. They enter into a drab inheritance themselves and look down condescendingly upon children who are far and away more alive than they are. Before they know where they are, they are wearing the bottoms of their trousers rolled and the delight and abandon have fled to be seen no more. I can't get through to people like that; they don't seem to be real people any longer; they have shrivelled. It happens to

100

all kinds of people—believers, I'm afraid, almost as much as unbelievers—and once it has happened it's a long job to put things right again.

If I'm to do my job I must be in the hands of people with open eyes. You don't need open eyes to look up a point in a reference book or a railway time-table; that's a purely mechanical operation. But you do need open eyes to read a book that is designed to expand your awareness and to help you see life from a new angle.

Have you ever noticed how Jesus appealed to the imagination and opened men's eyes to things they had never noticed or thought about? He didn't just hand out information. He made people think. He composed cryptic sayings and handed out conundrums to self-satisfied people. He put the Pharisees on the spot and made them painfully aware of the merciless end of their religious rules and regulations.[47] He embarrassed the rich young ruler by not giving him the answer he was hoping for.[48] He did what poets often do: he adopted an oblique approach and opened men's eyes by putting things in a different light—often by using metaphor.

The man who despises poetry misses a great deal of what I have to offer. He is sure to miss much that makes me valuable. He has probably missed what Shakespeare has to offer. He is a man to be pitied.

What's that story about the woman who looked at one of Turner's paintings? If I remember rightly, she said that *she* could never see such colours in the sky. To which Turner replied, "But don't you wish you could?" That's it. Exactly. I expect people to come to me with their eyes open (I'll open them still further), to be ready to receive new impressions, to explore as they read. I'm not asking too much, am I? After all, I think you human beings don't get much profit from Shakespeare or Milton unless you come to *Hamlet* or *Paradise Lost* in that frame of mind.

Usually people need some incentive to take on a piece of serious reading. Perhaps they see one of Shakespeare's plays performed, or they come across a quotation from Milton in an unexpected setting, and their curiosity is awakened. It is the job of the clergy to provide this kind of incentive in relation to me, and very good many of them are at doing it. In fact, until men and women have been woken up in this way, they hardly bother with me; they are apathetic.

At the other extreme are those who give me a very rough handling indeed because they have got a glint in their eye. They read me—true—but they hardly read anything else. They are so convinced of my importance that they dismiss every other expression of the human spirit as worthless. They in fact have an obsession about me, and an obsession about me is as unpleasant as an obsession about anything else.

Do you know, I value good humour and a sense of proportion. I like to deal with people who are balanced, poised and reasonable. It seems to me—and again, I say, I don't fully understand you human beings—that what distinguished the early Christian from the Greek pagan was not fanaticism or immoderate interest in religion as a special subject, but love, hope and faith.

I say again, it's a matter of imagination. To get the best out of me, you have to read me imaginatively—in the way you read poetry. You have to be open to new impressions. You have to explore as you read. You have to be prepared to see the truth about things—and that may mean seeing something you haven't seen before, or have never seen put in quite that way.

I know I'm asking for something that's far from easy. You human beings don't like being disturbed. If you have worked out a routine, you like to keep to it. If you have set opinions, you don't like having them upset. I know that the kind of reading I am asking for—creative reading, if I can call it that—is difficult, as difficult in its way as creative writing. Many people find it so hard that they give up. Their reading of the Bible becomes perfunctory; what began as an exciting exploration becomes a repetitive reading of familiar words. They know what's coming.

People who have had this disappointing experience tend to develop fixed ideas. They fall back on a few familiar aspects of the Gospel and can be relied upon to remind others of them whenever the opportunity presents itself. This gets them a bad name—and, what is worse, it gets me a bad name. I do not like getting a reputation for being a bore.

And nor, I may add, do I like to be the sort of book that people decide to plough through grimly, a few verses at a time, whether or not their interest is awakened. There's something humiliating about it—rather like being a set book. But there's no reason why I should be treated in this way. There are plenty of books about that can stimulate you human beings into an inquiring frame of mind about me. I can remember people coming to me itching to know what St Paul said about glory just because they had been reading C. S. Lewis. And I can think of others who couldn't wait to get me off the shelf on a Sunday to see whether what the preacher had said was really in the New Testament or not. Writers and preachers who have that effect on people are my strongest allies.

I ought to point out that the question of how much time a man spends reading me is of hardly any importance. I have known people who have spent an entire half-hour with me, but in fact have had merely one fantasy after another passing through their minds the whole time. I might as well have been miles away for all the good I was doing; they could have had their day-dreams without me. On the other hand I can remember occasions when a couple of minutes with me (of course the ground had been prepared) were enough to explode a lifelong assumption. It's a matter of coming to me with a prepared mind, I suppose. Given that, and a certain measure of obedience, I can make the most enormous changes.

I'm not a dull book, you know. My message had men skipping and dancing when it first broke upon the earth. But anything can be made dull if men bring listless, complacent minds to it. The more relentless Puritans used to turn me into a gloomy book about a gloomy Gospel. Better, they argued, to avoid all possible occasion of temptation than to jeopardise one's eternal salvation. And that sounds reasonable. But life is not so simple for you human beings. Before they knew where they were, those second-rank Puritans had turned themselves into the self-righteous, long-faced spoil-sports who meet you everywhere in the literature of the time.

I like to think about ducks.

Yes, ducks. You remember that F. W. Harvey described God

as creating comical things like ducks to prevent men's minds from becoming dull, humourless and glum. Ducks give you human beings a sense of proportion. They add a touch of gaiety to life. They do what Jesus often did. Serious as he was, he often rejoiced with those who rejoiced. He did not set out to eliminate pleasure from life. Indeed, he was accused, you remember, of being a glutton and a wine-bibber.[49]

Oh this lack of imagination! It meets you everywhere—in hymns, in church furniture, in preaching and teaching, everywhere.

It's lack of imagination that makes men attack the Gospels for being defective biographies. Men are familiar with the idea of a biography as such and they cannot bring themselves to accept that there may be another form altogether for dealing with a unique life like the life of Jesus. But the form lays emphasis exactly where it is needed, upon the ministry, death and resurrection of Jesus. For most purposes it does not make much difference whether or not a man believes that the sun actually stood still in the sky for Joshua in Old Testament days. But it does make a great deal of difference whether a man believes that Jesus came back from the dead. The resurrection is an endorsement of the claims that Jesus made during his life. To believe in the resurrection means believing that when Jesus forgave sins and altered the Jewish interpretation of the Law he was acting authoritatively. It means believing that Jesus was not a villain but the Son of God. It means that his teaching is not merely good advice but God's own interpretation of life. It means a new set of allegiances, a new scale of values. It means new men.

This is the whole point of me and my message—new men. To read me and fail to see this is to miss the point. It is like paying a visit to Brand's Hatch and not noticing the racing cars. It is like visiting Regent's Park Zoo and not noticing the animals. *Your* job requires you to keep your imagination alert; your clients would soon notice it if you failed to do that. But lots of people packed up their imagination years ago. Think about them sometimes, won't you. I know you get furious when you think of the ugliness with which men are contented in city streets and public places nowadays, but think of the drab lives many people are now living because their eyes are shut to the eternal things. You can help to open their eyes by showing them the things in their own streets that they have never noticed; by doing that you will be helping them to bring an alert imagination to *me*. The two things are connected, you know. So don't despair.

Chapter Twelve

Ask silly questions . . .

There's something I like about you. No, I'm not just flattering. I was going to say—before you interrupted me—that you bring an inquiring mind to me. I can always tell. Some people who come to me stopped asking questions long ago. Pure vegetable from the neck up. Very religious, mind you, but they long ago stopped asking questions. Some of them of course thought they knew all the answers—at least what they thought to be the important answers—already, so they just stopped inquiring any longer. Very boring for me. I know exactly how they are going to treat me.

But I never know with you. It depends whether you have just been reading L. P. Hartley's *The Hireling* or Alan Sillitoe's *The Loneliness of the Long Distance Runner*. It depends, too, whether you have been having a chat with that friend of yours who edits a motoring magazine or whether you have just come from the sailing club. You aren't predictable. You take an interest in things.

You're the kind of person I was really written for, it seems to me. I can get on with people who are asking questions or feeling their way towards asking questions. I can't do much with people who are in a rut and happy to remain in one rut or another. Perhaps it's because I have jerked so many people out of their settled ways in my time that I get impatient when I see men and women content with second best things. Nothing upsets me more than contented suburbanites who have lost interest in the important questions.

I can't pretend to know how you human beings come to

abandon the curiosity most of you were born with; perhaps it's something to do with the fact that you have to live by some kind of a routine—breakfast, dinner, tea, supper and so on. And some of you have to live the same dull life for forty years, I've noticed. That must be enough to quench anybody's curiosity. But I find myself growing more indignant, the older I get, when my readers rub along with a strictly limited curiosity about what makes people tick and how to solve the puzzle of human existence. Some people don't seem to find it a puzzle at all. They're quite happy with nine to five, telly in the evening, and two or three weeks on the Costa Brava each year.

I'm not in the least surprised when I hear about lively minds outside the Church preferring the company of other lively minds to the company of dull believers. It is unfortunate, to say the least, if any man has to choose between shallow faith and profound agnosticism.

Think for a moment of the contrast between E. M. Forster's *Howard's End* and the best evangelistic sermon you have heard. A thoughtful reader of the former will find it hard to be anything but severe with the latter, and this contrast must be borne in mind by anybody who is keen on evangelism as it is generally understood. The sermon can never come within a thousand miles of the subtlety of the novel and its grasp of all that is determinative, yet unsaid, about relations between human beings, yet the preacher (or perhaps, dare I say, the demagogue) is all too prone to suggest that the depth of the matter is on his side and that the other view of life is inadequate.

Readers who come to me with their minds alerted and made supple by books like *Howard's End*, *The Hireling*, Katherine Mansfield's short stories and John Wain's *The Smaller Sky* are ready to plumb the human predicament without expecting a string of foolproof answers. People like that have learned that life is not the simple matter it all too often appears in sermons and religious propaganda.

Often my highest task is to nerve men to face the truth about themselves. Self-deceptive and subtle as they know themselves to be, they find that reading me is like looking into a mirror. Remember, after all, how imaginatively and intriguingly—if I can put it like that—Jesus dealt with people. He did not talk to everybody in the same routine manner. You have only to think of his conversation with the woman at the well and his trouncing of the Pharisees. He responded to a witty reply such as the Syrophoenician woman gave him. He threw back questions to his questioners and handed out riddles to the self-assured. He brought men to face the truth about themselves (as Quive-Smith unwittingly brought the hero of Geoffrey Household's *Rogue Male* to face the truth about *him*self). Jesus did not hand out magic recipes which suited all cases. He treated men as individuals and dealt with the particular questions that were bothering them—and sometimes they themselves did not know what they were. This kind of perceptiveness is well understood by those who have been prompted and teased into an exploration of the human scene by poets, novelists and others who have gone through the world with their eyes open.

Don't mistake my meaning. I am not intending to imply that you must be a man of letters or a member of the *avant-garde* to have real faith in Christ. God does not confine his self-revelation to intellectuals; after all, the first disciples were not intellectuals. But people like you, with alert receptive minds, are trampling on God's gift to them if they quench their curiosity and ruin their mental agility. If you know what poets and others have understood about man, you will be better able to understand a Christ who entered into the depths of the human predicament.

I may appear to be an indifferently edited miscellany. My writers may have lacked style. But I think I may claim to be one of the biggest books in the world. For the size of books is not measured by the number of pages but by the scope and range of the subject. With respect, therefore, I am not a book to be handled lightly by little men with little minds. I deserve better treatment. I ask men to come to me with big questions and alert minds—and when men come like that they find themselves beginning to think differently about things.

But, as is true of other books, the man who comes to me with superficial questions will be able to take away superficial answers and feel that he has successfully come to grips with the matter. If you misuse me I don't complain—just as a Rolls-Royce doesn't

111

complain if you use it as a delivery van. But the man who uses a Rolls-Royce as a delivery van is telling you something about himself, whatever else he is doing.

Jesus did not encourage men to indulge their curiosity about the more remote aspects of God's arrangements for mankind. He did not enlighten them about the date of the Second Coming (though he did tell them how its imminence should affect their lives); he did not enlighten them about how many men would finally be saved (though he did urge his disciples to make sure that they themselves would be numbered amongst them). Idle speculation was not an appropriate response to Jesus' religious teaching; keen, committed interest in God's design was another matter. The parable of the sower puts clearly the outcome of superficial curiosity: the rapid growth of enthusiasm is followed by an equally rapid withering as the shallow soil is unable to fulfil its first promise.[50] Jesus discouraged superficial questions—questions about dividing an inheritance with a brother,[51] questions about who was the greatest among the disciples.[52] It was not until men came to ask the right questions that Jesus began the serious business of educating them.

As I was saying, it's funny how people—Christians, many of them call themselves—stop asking questions, or ask silly ones. They have made what is I am afraid the common mistake of thinking that because they have had their sins forgiven they know the answers to all the important questions already. They're too busy answering questions they think other people are asking to have any time for listening. People like that give others the impression that Christianity is talk, talk, talk.

Sometimes they also give the impression that to be a believer means to sit in judgement on other people. As though any one of you human beings can know all about another human being's circumstances or difficulties! It's not only people who call themselves Christians who read me, remember; it often surprises me that there are people who take me quite seriously and yet will have nothing at all to do with any religious institutions. I wouldn't presume to explain their motives, but I respect them for whatever good actions they do as a result of my prompting and I am sure you do.

But I know of some people who have an unlovely habit of putting labels on people, of saying that some people are "converted" and others are not. This kind of talk would not be heard at all if people paid attention to me. As I said earlier, I just don't divide people in that way, and I am not very fond of loose talk about conversion. I do distinguish between the baptized and the unbaptized[53] and I am interested in whether a man is living out the meaning of his baptism,[54] but I have no interest in the jargon by which a particular group recognises members and non-members.

People who make a habit of putting labels on others have only a very superficial acquaintance with me. I am not concerned with getting people to say the right thing, to use the accepted terminology and generally to conform to the pattern approved by a religious club. That kind of thing doesn't appeal to me at all. Have you noticed how reluctant Jesus was to categorise people, particularly to allow a superior standing to those who claimed to have Abraham for their father?[55] He spoke ambiguously about those who were for him and those who were against him. And have you noticed how the Church of my day was full of what you might call half-believers, sincere inquirers and misguided enthusiasts as well as ripe men and women in Christ? I'm thinking of people like Apollos and the believers in Galatia and Thessalonica. As I understand the matter it is a ludicrous over-simplification to divide the world into Christians and non-Christians, whether you make baptism or a conversion-story the basis of the division. God looks on the heart, and only God can gauge the sincerity and acceptability of another man's faith in Christ.

This business of labelling becomes even more misleading when it is applied to corporate bodies. To ask whether a firm or company is "Christian", for example, is to ask a question that is not very meaningful. An individual may be a Christian (though, as I have said, I am not very fond of that term), and a number of individuals in positions of responsibility may be Christians, but there is no criterion that I am aware of for deciding whether a board of directors, for example, is "Christian". In an extreme form the matter was once highlighted by the person who advanced the view that the South African government is the most

Christian government in the world because nearly all its members are churchgoers. This is the kind of silly answer you get when you allow yourself to ask silly questions. Instead of asking whether a government or a board of directors is "Christian", it is better and more useful to ask whether the members act responsibly and justly and whether they value *people*.

Asking silly questions—of course, all this began with the disciples and *their* silly questions. They would ask Christ if they might sit at his side when he came into his kingdom. They would ask permission to send down fire upon cities that treated him with scant respect. They would ask how many times they had to forgive somebody who offended them and then came back to apologise. Can you think of any questions sillier than those! But there's this to encourage you. If Jesus could transform cloddish men like that, he can do the same for the pedestrian and short-sighted members of your rather ugly and insipid society.

I get quite used to people missing my point. It's a familiar experience for me to see a man or a woman walking away from me with a complacent expression on his or her face. I know that they have misunderstood something of mine and gone away justifying themselves about some pattern in their lives.

Of course, some will say that to miss my point is an indication that you do not possess the Spirit of God and therefore cannot discern things that are spiritually discerned. Undoubtedly there is truth in the view that you human beings cannot see spiritually until your eyes have been opened,[56] but it is not at this deep level that failure to see the point frequently occurs. Often it happens through laziness or mental inertia, just as people have misunderstood More's *Utopia* (a tongue-in-cheek book if ever I saw one), or tried to tack happy endings on to Shakespeare's tragedies.

The plain fact of the matter is that you human beings love to trivialise. I sometimes wonder whether you are worth bothering about—nothing personal, you understand. But to be asked silly questions, to listen to the prattle of empty minds, to hear people bickering over what I really mean! No wonder I sometimes cut up!

Well, I expect I have made myself plain. If you human beings

114

allow the tough way of life described in my pages to degenerate into a routine of bazaars in the parish hall, women's meetings, an entertaining procession of visiting speakers and inexorable attempts to improve on last year's figures for this and that, you have only yourselves to blame. I am simply not concerned with these things. I stick to the main point, and so should you. But it seems that sticking to the main point is so painful for you—in terms of heartache, concentration and disagreements—that you are tempted to reduce the operation to manageable proportions, to avoid controversial issues, to choose easier objectives than you ought, and finally to keep the whole operation inside the church and the church hall. Many local churches do operate this kind of restricted programme. Obedience to the Gospel comes to seem merely a matter of attending whatever happens to be going on in the church hall at any given time. Good Christians are those who attend the functions; bad Christians are those who do not.

You smile. But this is the kind of impression a church often gives.

Think of it in this way. If Jesus were alive today you would take your most serious questions to him. You would regard it as a unique opportunity to hear his views on the matters that perplex you most. Well, you can find God speaking to you in my pages. You must set your clearest views on the important subjects alongside me and be prepared to change your views as a result. Instead of looking to me to reinforce your prejudices (whether those prejudices are social, political or economic) you must be ready to see things differently. You must be prepared to forsake the accepted orthodoxy of your particular group if your reading of my pages indicates that such dissent is required. You should in any case be prepared to accept that life is too complex to be reduced to a few headings with authoritative answers supplied in kit form.

Chapter Thirteen

Now give me a chance

Well, this is going to be our last conversation, so I'll try to make the most of it. You have been very patient with me and I know that sometimes you haven't by any means agreed with what I've said, but you have allowed me to speak without interruption and I'm grateful for that. If you had realised what a drubbing you used to give me in the days when you couldn't resist telling me what was what! Perhaps you're better at listening now you're older.

Now, what was I going to say? Ah, yes. I know. I was going to suggest that now we've cleared the ground between us you might like to give me a chance. Not just you yourself—you and your friends, of course.

You will have gathered already that I don't want you to rush to reinstate, as it were, the Church of my day. For one thing, as we have said, it is not clear what the Church was like then, and for another thing, it is not clear that God's purpose is a perpetuation of any particular moment in the history of the Church.

No, the first thing I ask of you is this. Please give me freedom to have my own effect. Don't be too sure you know what will follow when people read me as though for the first time. I'm sure Erasmus didn't know what effect would follow from his editing my text afresh and making me generally available. But as they say, Erasmus laid the egg and Luther hatched it. You never know; there may be developments such as you could never anticipate.

So if I lead you on to something quite new, don't be surprised.

My job is not to support preconceived notions and bolster existing organisations. You and your friends may find me upsetting both if you give me half a chance. But I can't upset anything if I'm ill-used and badly treated. That's the point I've been trying to make during our conversations. It's because I'm ignored, distorted, over-simplified and asked silly questions that you members of the Church often get misleading ideas and go the wrong way about things. What I'm asking you to do is to let me speak for myself, to let me come out from under the load of misrepresentation that you human beings have heaped upon me.

I'm asking you to do some quite definite things. I'm asking you to remove the moss, debris and clutter so that my original shape and texture are apparent. Then I am asking you to take off the tinted and dusty spectacles through which you have been accustomed to look at me. I know it may be painful for eyes which have become habituated to subdued tones and soft outlines to be confronted with sharp distinctions and stunning colours, but I am afraid you must brace yourself for the task. Otherwise you are only looking at me in disguise. I take it the great painters of the past did not intend their works to be seen in a dimmed and darkened condition, and it is fair to assume that my compilers did not intend *me* to fade and grow blunted over the years.

It's no good, however, letting me be seen for what I am if you are not going to take any notice of what I say. There's this matter of obedience, as I've mentioned before. I'll do all I can to help you—remember, I'm never so happy as when I am being continually thumbed through to provide practical guidance on day-to-day problems—but you'll have to bring your professional skill and experience to bear on many of them before you can get a satisfactory answer. And then you'll have to see that things get done as a result. For my part, provided you stop misusing me, you can use me as much as you like and I shan't complain. I simply enjoy wearing out.

On some matters, of course, I prove uncomfortably precise and entirely predictable. Everybody knows my position on such matters as patience and a forgiving spirit, for example. Again, what I have to say about repenting and believing will never prove very surprising to any reader. If men would concentrate on obeying my injunctions in these respects, they would have a development programme to last them the rest of their lives.

But there is a wide range of questions on which the individual believer is not only expected but encouraged to make up his own mind, and it is here that the points I have been making will come into their own. Your generation has problems on a scale unknown to previous generations. Many of the problems you face can be solved only by men of different skills working in teams; many of the problems are economic, for example, and call for experts in a number of fields. The position today is that men and women in Christ have the opportunity of utilising the skills they have and the guiding principles they find in my pages to serve God and their fellow-men. What is needed is resourceful, skilful, adaptable men and women—and this is just the kind of men and women envisaged by my writers.

The outcome of the Gospel, it seems, is intended to be an immense variety. To become a man or woman in Christ is not to become a dull conformist, but to develop a unique personality, to blossom, to discover new potentialities. When the individual believer comes to me humbly, inquiringly, ready to receive fresh light from God's Word and act upon it, things start happening, unpredictable things. The reader finds he has something to live for, something to fire his imagination, something for his hands to do. He begins to ask what it means to be a man in Christ and how a man in Christ fulfils his domestic, economic and social responsibilities. The mass conditioning of your society fails to quench the initiative of the new man in Christ. He is getting his orders from the Top Authority.

You'll notice that I described such a man as asking what he should do as a man in Christ rather than as a Christian. This won't surprise you, but I should like to underline the difference. People who ask questions the way I ask them, people who use my terminology and speak my language often find that things appear in a new light straightaway. The word "Christian" is a straightforward label. Before the person who uses it realises what is happening, he is thinking in individualistic terms and reducing the whole matter of knowing God to the holding of certain opinions. If instead he thinks about "men in Christ" he is compelled to consider matters in a much larger frame of reference. He is continually reminded that God is greater than he is and that there is room for more than just himself in this new sphere. He gets a new perspective and takes a new view of a number of familiar matters.

As a result, a man may find himself obliged to alter his scale of priorities. He may begin to think more about his responsibilities as a husband and father and less about church meetings; the result may well be that he will make time for the encouragement and supervision of his children and let other things go. A man may also decide to spend more time on gaining qualifications which will enable him to make the most of his talents and do better at his daily work.

You may think I'm quibbling when I talk about the difference between asking what it means to be a Christian and asking what it means to be a man in Christ. But I don't think I am. After all, every subject has its distinctive vocabulary. If you are a mechanic, you have to think in terms of gear ratios, etc.; if you are a chemist you have to think in terms of hydrocarbons, etc. Whatever your interest is, you have to learn a distinctive vocabulary and get into the habit of using precise definitions. I've been present at too many study groups and discussions round a coffee-table to be unaware of what happens when you don't define your terms. If half a dozen people are talking about being a Christian, as often as not there will be half a dozen different ideas about what a Christian actually is. The vagueness is reduced immediately (so, probably, is the cosiness), the moment you start talking about men and women in Christ, or men and women who are baptized. After all, there's no special merit in vagueness. A man does not give up thinking precisely when he is impelled by the Holy Spirit; he is rather to think more justly, more exactly—and more imaginatively—than he did before.

The result of using my terms in this way should be that you men and women in Christ will come to be more purposeful than you are at present. You will have clearer and more precise goals; you will probably have different priorities; and you will be prepared to see your obedience to Christ expressed in terms of your responsibilities as employers, employees, citizens and husbands and wives rather than in terms of keeping obsolete Church organisations going.

Changes will take place inside the Church. My experience is that baptized people (or men and women in Christ, or any other of my expressions which you prefer) tend to be as conservative as other people; they do things the way they have always been done in their particular group—according to the prayer book, or according to the Schofield Bible, or according to Billy Graham. It often happens that Church leaders meet together to discuss large general issues such as communication, the role of the laity, and evangelism; and when the conference is over, they go back to do exactly what they were doing before. They are prepared for change but only within a carefully defined area. It is as though they have never considered the possibility that it is the framework, not the activities within the existing framework, that needs reconstruction. It is like dramatists meeting to discuss new developments in drama, but only considering developments that are possible in the context of a conventional stage with a proscenium arch. In fact I believe that present-day dramatists and theatre-goers are often far more flexible in their outlook than church-goers.

There's very little that I have to say on the way your generation should organise the Church; that is something for you to decide in the light of prevailing conditions. I must admit that I'm slightly amazed that you find it necessary to make so few changes at the present time, and I think that if you took me seriously you would certainly not be content to let things go on as they are at present. The practical details, however, are for you to settle. Again, you must use your own judgement.

My message is intended (amongst other things) to fire the imagination of a human being like you. It must be given the chance to do so. It therefore has to be presented in such a way as to leave room for an imaginative response. And sometimes this is just not possible in the existing set-up. To impose a pattern of Church life on the Gospel, to hedge its proclamation round with patterns that prevent that kind of response from emerging, is to thwart the end in view. How often have I seen people sitting silently under a sermon and leaving church immediately afterwards! That gives no opportunity for imaginative response. Indeed, a Church with rigid organisational forms discourages any such response from shaping itself. And this is one of the matters *you* will have to consider in *your* local church.

Think how differently things are done in other situations. In the class-room, I believe, a boy is given the opportunity of responding in his own way to the stimulating material put before him. He learns by his mistakes. He experiments. He masters the subject as he becomes mastered by it. It is this kind of learning situation, personal inquiry, personal response and the guidance of a more experienced person, that is urgently needed in the Church rather than a programme of handing answers and orthodoxy to people on a plate. I'm all for orthodoxy, but orthodoxy without vitality and honest response makes me shudder.

Of course, you lay people are often seriously at fault because you allow the clergy to get on with things as best they can. You cannot expect the Church to be functioning healthily if it is monopolised by the clergy, and it is people like you who must bring their experience to bear on the organising of the Church. It's all there in my pages if you care to look. Nobody could say I favour clerical dictatorship.

This question of lay responsibility is one that you will have to consider far more closely if you take me seriously. While congregational responsibility is confined to the maintenance of the church building and the purchase of new hymn books, you won't get mature believers. If you read what St Paul wrote to the Corinthians about saints judging the world, you won't hesitate to agree that men and women in Christ are expected to exercise an independent judgement. You may not think it possible or desirable to give a local church a free hand in ordering its worship and taking steps towards Church unity, but until something like this comes about, talk about lay responsibility will be so much hot air.

Remember, the Church of my day won through against Jewish opposition, against government suspicion, against intellectual contempt, because its members were full of the Holy Spirit and

124

because it understood its opponents' views as well as they understood them themselves. There really is no other way open to the members of the Church today. Nowadays, I understand, the Church cannot dictate policy; it can no longer rest on privileges; it must justify its views in the open market. Paul asked no better opportunity than this; nor should you.

Let me end this conversation of ours by saying this. It may sound presumptuous, but I think you will find that when I am set free and allowed to rule the Church in all its aspects, the result will be a Church quick to innovate, eager to exploit opportunities, ready for reform and keen to enlarge its understanding. My guess is that you will see a Church flexible rather than hidebound, adaptable rather than rigidly conformist, risk-taking rather than timid, practical rather than academic. A Church renewed after this manner will have an engaging way of suspecting its own assumptions and being sceptical about its own traditions. Such a Church will not only throw up men with ideas; it will pay attention to them. The result will be an unpredictable, galvanising, go-getting, stinging—and sometimes disappointing—fellowship that is a constant amazement to the world and to believers alike.

So give me a chance and see what we can do together.

New Testament references

1. Heb 4.12
2. Acts 5. 1–5
3. Acts 19. 11, 12
4. I Cor 8
5. I Cor 11. 3–16
6. Acts 15. 36–41
7. Acts 18. 24–28
8. e.g. I Cor 1. 12; 3. 5, 6
9. Gal 2. 11, 12
10. I Cor 15. 29
11. I Cor 11. 22
12. I Cor 1. 11, 12
13. Acts 6. 1–6
14. Matt 17. 24–27
15. Matt 21. 18–22
16. e.g. Matt 10. 28; 23. 33
17. Mark 10. 45
18. I Cor 14. 26
19. Mark 14. 22–25
20. e.g. Rom 5
21. Rom 6. 1–11
22. Rom 8. 9–11
23. Matt 20. 1–16
24. e.g. I Cor 14. 33–35
25. Matt 7. 12
26. Matt 7. 13, 14
27. Matt 25. 31–46
28. Eph 2. 11–22
29. II Cor 6. 17
30. Phil 1. 9, 10
31. I Cor 12. 28 (R S V)
32. Acts 9. 2
33. Acts 9. 14
34. Acts 6. 7
35. Phil 3. 12
36. I Tim 1. 13
37. II Cor 12. 2
38. Acts 2. 38
39. Mark 5. 1–13
40. Matt 8. 5–13
41. Mark 7. 24–30
42. Acts 10
43. John 1. 29
44. Mark 2. 23–3. 6
45. Luke 14. 28–33
46. Acts 17. 16–34
47. Matt 12. 9–14
48. Mark 10. 17–22
49. Matt 11. 19
50. Mark 4. 1–20
51. Luke 12. 13, 14
52. Mark 9. 33–37
53. Act 2. 41
54. Romans 6. 1–14
55. Matt 3. 9
56. I Cor 2. 14